Light Language Emerging

Light Language Emerging helps to bring understanding to a vast, new, and unusual subject: the language of light. When it spontaneously started happening to me many years ago, I had no exposure to it, no one to turn to and no immediate answers. A book like this is not only a catalyst for opening, but it becomes a life line for those having unique experiences as their telepathic communications begin to activate. With Yvonne's book, readers will come to understand their own multi-dimensional nature, their cosmic connection to their galactic family, and their ability to expand beyond limiting perceptions of self and life.

~ Jamye Price, light language channel, healer and teacher

Light Language Emerging

Activating Ascension Codes and Integrating Body, Soul, and Spirit

Yvonne Perry

Cover design by Emily Singleton. Layout by Rick Chappell.

ISBN-10: 098906882X
ISBN-13: 978-0-9890688-2-6
Write On! Publishing
Nashville, Tennessee
March 2014

http:// WeAre1inSpirit.com

Disclaimer: This book contains the opinions and thoughts of its author and is not intended to provide professional services or medical/psychological advice. The publisher/author claims no responsibility or liability for loss or risk incurred as a result of the use or application of any of the contents of the book. This book is not intended for making diagnoses or treatment of any illness. Contact your healthcare professional if you need help with a health issue.

Dedication

To all those who are in service to the light and love of Creator/Creatrix, my deepest heartfelt joy and appreciation that you are assisting us in this time of ascension!

Contents

Acknowledgments

We all have a piece to the ascension puzzle—no one possesses all the truth about everything there is. If one person exclusively held all knowledge, that person would be indispensible. I thank my team, which extends far beyond those mentioned here—some are in body and some in the higher dimensions—for their contributions to this project.

Much appreciation to Caron Goode and Cayce Shostak, who reminded me that I had said "yes" on a galactic level to writing this book.

Thank you to those who shared their stories, photos, art, or samples of written light language: Alison Hodgson, Amenreu, Angi Gaian Progeny, Astelle Anomellarun, Betsy Nelson, Brenda Williams, Diana Morningstar, Dr. Arthur Cushman, Dr. Salo Stanley, Emily Singleton, Jamye Price, Jennifer Hall, Jess Bray, Joan Kuykendall, Kelly Beavers, Maryanne Savino, Mazuin Mynrose, Randall Hawk, Teri Jo Tinus, Vara Humphreys, and Veronica O'Grady.

Thanks to Emily Singleton for creating the beautiful art for the book cover, and Rick Chappell for providing layout.

Foreword

By Amenreu

It is difficult, like anything else in the metaphysical world, to discuss the nature of a language by means of another language. It seems that there is always such a high potential for a loss in translation when regarding the spiritual world. So much so that the topic always comes up short of its true nature and power. I cannot explain in perfect experience that which I have found to be true regarding higher vibrational (light) language, but I can, with confidence, know that as the discussion begins to unfold, the potential for a remarkable shift is eminent with even the slightest conception of understanding on the part of a reader.

That's really how any metaphysical "thing" works, on the principal of the power of a single miniscule idea. Ideas are the fundamental seeds for manifestation. All it takes is the notion of a possibility, and the potentiality that a mind can create out of pure will or desire for the greatest possible outcome, to set into motion a galaxy of change within ourselves and in those around us. Light language is a mere facet of those creations, but with it comes the greatest potential for communication with our true nature, and since we are God or our own internal domain, none other than ourselves could truly understand the full nature of our own light language.

I wouldn't be able to accurately depict my first experience with light language, as the potential for the language began with the birth of my soul. I believe, or rather am shown to believe, that our soul (light) language begins with ourselves, with the birth of our souls, and if anyone could tell me when or how the birth of a soul happens, then I would be able to accurately tell you the birth of the language. Until then, I can only assume that the language is eternal and infinite, and unidentifiable, really, with any other soul's language. I am shown to believe that the nuts and bolts of light language are really our manifested form's attempt at describing the experience of having a lifeline to God through our cognitive vibration.

We are God, and we are human. And, that dual experience tries to output as sound, like vowels and consonants, and in patterns, like words and phrases. That's because there are patterns and cycles in our experiences. But, how with any human tongue could we really describe or define those patterns and cycles, or those experiences for that matter? It's like we are on this Earth to experience this world and share in these experiences; but, we are left without the means to really articulate those experiences to one another. It's as if we can have grand experiences with each other but only truly hold the joy of those experiences internally. It is the need or desire to attempt to articulate the joy I have in my spiritual experiences that drives my relationship with light language.

Few have seen the language in which I write, however, those who have seen it share the consensus: "I can't understand it, or know what it says, but I can feel it." Light language is a feeling experience, not a deciphering one. It's not a putting together of symbols and creating consistent meanings for those symbols; it's an empathetic absorption of another's experiencing of language. ("Empathy," the lost art of actually acknowledging that a soul exists in each of us instead of seeing the people that surround as emotionless meat sacks, but that's a whole other conversation.) It takes empathy to be able to communicate back and forth between experiencing souls—except that it doesn't really seem to be a communication. It's more of a resounding honoring of each other's experiences. That is perhaps why I don't communicate to very many in this language, or why I had this language as a spiritual tool for four years before I've even discussed it in depth or tried to reflect on it. The language that I share with God is an internal safety mechanism that I can always count on to know that I am, the I AM that is God. When I know this, there *is* nothing else. The language is my mantra to eternal peace in knowing that I am all that needs to be. Perhaps when I share that with the world, there is fear that doubt and hate and misunderstanding in another person will lead to the destruction of my own internal spiritual experience. It seems that destruction is at the forefront of humanity's goals on this Earth. We destroy hope well, and we destroy each other well. Perhaps this language is an evolutionary process to help us transcend the need for destruction, and replace it with the joy of creation.

When I experience writing or speaking this language, I disappear from this world as a being who needs to understand that which surrounds him, and I am replaced by a potential to create closer to or further away from that which is already manifested (we call it reality). Reality, the culmination of the most appropriate probability given the equation of all the energies provided and their adjacent power of will combined with the chosen perspective of all souls at once—this is not a façade, it is a creation. Reality is the best case scenario given, infinity divided into perspectives to the infinite degree. And yet reality moves. Reality changes, maybe slowly, but it does move; it evolves, so then does the best-case scenario. This human moment is real, and the next moment is real, but those moments at their core are really the same moment, because they are rooted in the awareness that a moment *can* be perceived. And when there is awareness, there is peace. When there is the ability to have awareness, regardless of the scenery, peace can be had everywhere and in all moments. And since the potential for this awareness is inconceivable but probably infinite, that awareness must already be, and it must always be. And thus, we find God.

The ability to behold peace is that of an individual's experience, but the ability to manifest peace is the decision of the masses. The masses may be influenced, but swayed only by their desire to be aware of peace, and for their neighbor to also be aware of peace.

These words are a manifestation of the connection I have to God; they are not meant to be possessed. Therefore, they are not mine, but they are for my lips to speak and my hands to write. Thus, is the language of light.

As I write from this space of peace, I do not recognize this voice, this man, for he is not a man; he is a being and he is divinity. And that being of divinity is a message from God declaring that there has never been, nor ever will be, a space where peace cannot be found.

Introduction

I awoke at 12:43 on the morning of November 23, 2013 from a dream in which I had told some close friends goodbye. I heard almost audibly, "It's time for me to leave." Then there was a swoosh that sounded like one of those plastic cylinders going up the vacuum chute at a bank's drive-through. LavendarRose had left the building/body. And, all the negative mental chatter I had been wrestling with for the past year was gone as well. All I felt, besides some confusion as to why LavendarRose had walked out and *who* had walked in, was peaceful.

Like I always do when I think I'm having a soul exchange or significant soul shift, I contacted my psychologist friend, Dr. Caron Goode. I knew she would be able to "read" my energy and tell me what was going on. She saw me completely surrounded by and floating in a cloud of blue starlight dust. I was resting peacefully and lying still while receiving a rewiring of my brain, nervous system, and neural pathways. She said it could take up to a year to complete this process. In the top of my head Caron saw a triangular-shaped opening through which I was receiving downloads of information. Through that same portal, I was also transmitting a frequency that was issuing a signal to starseeds from other planetary systems. I was letting them know that it was time for them to come to Earth and help with the next phase of the ascension of humanity. She also told me I would be writing another book—several more, in fact.

When I shared my experience with Cayce Shostak, co-host of a monthly conference call in which she and I provide coaching for starseeds, she also came up with the message that I would be writing a new book. I didn't see how that would be possible any time soon. I could not sit at the computer for more than thirty minutes without spiking a headache and increasing the pain resulting from a head injury and whiplash that occurred less than two months prior. I had torn muscles, ligaments, and tissues in my neck and back. How could I possibly write a book with this physical condition? Since it was the holiday season I bah-hum-bugged Cayce's notion and put it on the back burner next to Caron's.

Back in August of 2011, I had an oversoul visitation during which I enjoyed twelve days of bliss and constantly smelled an angelic fragrance that no one else smelled (clairolfactance). When that heavenly fragrance came back December 4, 2013 and lasted for nine days, I knew it meant something significant was occurring for me. The last time this mysterious aroma came, I started writing *Shifting into Purer Consciousness*. I don't know why I thought I had retired from writing about my personal experiences, researching, interviewing people, and being put through a wringer of spiritual growth. I was enjoying my season of rest required to heal a concussion. I had even stopped resisting and thinking I needed to be out of bed and doing something more useful.

The day after Christmas I awoke at 3 a.m., hearing light language in my head. I felt compelled to speak it, so I began to whisper. Then, I had the urge to speak it aloud. As the vibration came forth, I realized there was something important being said, which I understood at a soul level. I sensed that I was to ask others to speak light language; so, I posted an announcement on Facebook and thought that was that. I was done, right? Obviously, not. I had fifteen responses in about as many minutes. People were sharing their experiences and wanted more information about this phenomenon. I collected the responses and contacted several people privately. They had stories worth telling so I wrote what I thought was an article. I was ready to share it publically when more information started coming in. The next thing I knew my article had grown to five-thousand words and I thought, *I may be writing a book.* Sneaky, very sneaky, how the Universe drew me into this project. But then, I got excited and started interviewing more people and asking them about their experience with light language. That led to the creation of the book you are now reading.

Each of us has our own truth. If your truth is like mine, it is malleable, rather than fixed in stone. My truth changes as downloads and new revelations are given to me either in my dream state, after speaking, signing, or writing in light language, or through my daily experiences. Our collective consciousness is changing as our beliefs, thoughts, and patterns are transforming to allow the body to shift out of its dense state and embody more of our higher or divine self. I would not want to be stuck in one belief system or be bound to what I believed yesterday. It is this kind of openness that allows us to make changes and progress in our personal ascension. Therefore, what you have read in some of my previous books may be different from what you read in this book. For starters, I now believe that I have had several walk-ins and my body serves as a host to several souls in a soul group with a common mission. They come in and out of my body or field as needed to complete certain tasks. This is likely why the fragrance comes when I'm going to write a book—that soul essence is part of my soul group.

So, if LavendarRose left in a *swoosh* in November, who is in my body now? This soul must be the one who owns the fragrance—that's my truth for now, although it does not explain why the fragrance left after nine days this time. I call her "76-99" because I continually smelled this same etheric fragrance between 1976 and 1999; and, there are indicators that she was in my body then and has returned to complete the next segment of this mission. I now sense that 76-99 was the oversoul who draped over me in 2011. She had come back from her mission during which she sat in council meetings and discussions with starseeds in other planetary systems who agreed and are preparing to come to Earth at this time. Those souls will be arriving en mass in 2014. In fact, many of them are already on the planet and you may be one of them.

The placeholder soul, LavendarRose, was in my body for almost fourteen years and became strongly attached to Earth life, so much so that she lost perspective of the big picture. She did not want to give up her position when 76-99 was ready to reclaim the driver's seat in 2011. In fact, she refused to have a soul exchange at that time, yet I sensed that was what was being requested. Thus, the "intervention" at IKEA in October 2013 disconnected her from the body and allowed 76-99 to come back in.

I figured all this out when Casey and I were on the phone briefing for the December Walk-ins Among Us Group Conference Call that we cohost each month. She read a question from our itinerary to see which one of us would address that topic. I heard her ask something completely different. I thought she asked how my new walk-in soul was integrating. Somehow that led me to hear Cayce ask if I had had a soul exchange prior to the one in 1999. I immediately got an image of myself in 1976 when I was burned. During that near-death experience, I simultaneously saw two perspectives of what was happening. One consciousness or soul was floating near the ceiling looking down on the scene and the other was seeing the situation unfold as she sat in a puddle of flames, unable to get up and out of the burning house. She knew she was about to "die" and even saw her obituary in the newspaper. To this day, I still have both of those perspectives etched in my mind and can recall them vividly. It occurred to me that the reason I had both of those perspectives is because there was a soul coming into the body and a soul about to leave. My natal or born-in soul did not fragment during that episode—she walked out and 76-99 walked in. Even though I was experiencing the pain and trauma of being severely burned, I was able to comfort and assure my mother that I was going to be just fine and that there was nothing to worry about. She arrived from work at the ER while the nurses were debriding charred skin from my right hand. So, this new information, which I don't know how I missed all these years, brings my walk-ins to a count of three, that I know of.

While this book is not about my walk-in events or other soul experiences, I feel I need to interweave my stories (and those of other people) into the topic of this book—light language. Many people are having soul shifts, getting soul upgrades, receiving downloads of high-vibrating energy, being visited by future selves, or integrating higher aspects of their soul. These look similar to a walk-in experience in which a completely different soul (usually from your soul family or guidance team) switches places with the soul currently in the body. I hope to help you see how light language plays a role in activating and integrating these kinds of experiences.

The 76-99 soul is the one who originally activated light language in this body in 1994. The writing of this book, and the activations that it carries, are part of her mission to bring forth oneness, unity, and a better understanding of our multidimensional souls. It only makes sense that she, having a keen interest in the gifts of the spirit, would desire to bring forth this body of information to activate others and prepare them to embody more evolved soul aspects by speaking in light language. This book is to help people, like you, who are hearing a new language that, while it sounds strange, "feels" familiar. You may have been speaking or singing these new sounds and wondering what affect they are having. You may have questions that this book will answer.

The starseeds that came in the 1980s and 1990s were like transponders, emitting an identifying signal in response to a received signal. We are like a communications satellite, gathering signals over a range of frequencies and re-transmitting them on a different set of downlink frequencies to receivers on Earth. The early starseed walk-ins cleared a path that would allow the upgrades needed for human ascension to come online. We also acted (and still do) like test subjects to see how the upgrades would play out in the human form. These early walk-ins are now receiving upgrades on a wide scale, and there is a new influx of starseeds being called in through the transmission of encoded light language.

Light language is sacred geometry in vibrational form. We can feel the sweet vibration washing over our body and soul when we speak, sing, hear, write, dance, sign, or intone it. Since it is creative energy, light language can be used to manifest or speak into form what is held as a thought or intention. It can also heal the body, raise the vibration of a soul, and open/reactivate new strands of DNA that scientists have referred to as "junk" DNA. I have seen the practice of speaking light language create a shift in consciousness, increase empathic abilities and psychic gifts, facilitate amazing emotional breakthroughs, and heal the body of illness/suffering. In recent years, this language has been emerging in people who are having a spiritual awakening. In this book, I will share a few stories from people I interviewed. Perhaps its message will lead you to your blissful destiny as a spirit being having a human expression on Earth. Hopefully, it will be gentler and with less pain, suffering, and inconvenience than I have experienced this past year!

I am about to take your soul on a journey that will blow your logical mind. The things presented in this book may cause your ego to rare up and question whether or not I am sane. There have been times when I questioned whether any of this is real, but I assure you that my experiences are not much different than what others are experiencing during this age of enlightenment. This book contains a transmission of grace through light language that has been part of my journey in integrating aspects of my soul. As you read what has come to me in "unusual" ways, you will move beyond this 3-D reality and step into a realm behind the veil to your star origins. Your soul will be awakened, inspired, and thrilled at what you discover. These discoveries are not really new; you will simply begin to remember what you already know.

Souls speak the Creator's language of light. You speak it regardless of whether or not you realize it. I will show you what light language is and how to listen for it in your everyday life through images, dreams, visions, nature sounds, art, movement, body sensations, and conversations with other light beings. If you already have a light language, you will begin to speak it with new understanding and added dialects; and, you will have a better appreciation for its purpose. By doing so, some lost part of you will come home to a place it really never left.

Chapter 1 ~ Restoring Divine Communication

Aspects of our soul are scattered throughout the Universe in multiple dimensions, including simultaneous Earth incarnations. Multidimensional selves or aspects are like a three-way mirror that you may see in a dressing room. As you stand in front of the triple mirror, your image is duplicated endlessly. However, rather than being identical, each aspect of your soul has its own distinct personality. They may take different forms that allow them to live in environments or dimensions/octaves that are unlike those found on Earth. The characteristics or features of each one may look different, but it is still *you* being reflected across the spectrum of no-time-no-space.

> *For now we see only a reflection as in a mirror; then we shall see face to face. Now I know in part; then I shall know fully, even as I am fully known. (I Corinthians 13:12)*

The more evolved aspects vibrate at a purer, more loving frequency and may actually be assisting you as guides on your current journey. Some soul aspects may have fragmented through traumatic experiences. In fact, the entire Divine Feminine aspect of the trinity was fragmented by dark forces eons ago and we are reclaiming this aspect into our bodies, the earth, and all creation now. Because they have been stripped of their light, these fragmented aspects may appear as part of our lesser-loved shadow side. To think in terms of higher and lower, good and bad, is actually duality thinking. As members of the planetary ascension team, we are not here to discard duality but to embrace it, acknowledge it, and honor it and then make the individual choice that everything in our lives is *for* us, not *against* us or happening *to* us. Bringing the duality together in wholeness balances masculine and feminine principles/energies.

The ascension is about wholeness. In order to create cohesion among soul aspects, all these soul aspects are being collected, healed, and integrated as they form a unified expression of the soul. This does not mean they will be uniform, undifferentiated, or have only one personality or style. The beautiful diversity, skills, talents, and gifts that each of these aspects has to offer will be retained in a harmonious symphony as they come together in oneness to manifest of love and goodness, within and without.

Oneness means we see the best in ourselves and others while honoring all soul aspects without judgment. This happens when we consciously make non-resistant choices that support the highest and best in everyone, everything, and every situation. Unfortunately, due to our programming, it has been difficult for us to consistently do this in the past. Fortunately, our programming is changing through the upgrades that have been made in the human template. We are now able to more easily access our divinity in a tangible way and it is making a difference in how our minds, emotions, and bodies function. Light language is one of the ways we access these upgrades and bring them into our daily experience.

Even though we are multidimensional beings with many levels of awareness, the body has been functioning with only a small amount of the soul actually inside of it. The purest aspect of our soul cannot live in the typical human body at our current level of evolution. The merkabah is the mechanism or vehicle that allows the physical human body to convert from a dense form into a lighter form that is able to house all aspects of the soul in a unified manner and travel into other dimensions. The ongoing restoration process of the light-body is essential to the ascension of humanity as we are creating the New Earth. The body is changing into a crystalline structure that can live in a higher vibration, but we are not going to fly away and leave the earth. The earth is ascending into higher dimensions and we are going with her. This transformation requires a rewiring and reprogramming of the DNA that will result in a molecular reconstruction of the body.

This molecular reconstruction relates to how the form or body holds space on Earth, as well as how it houses the soul or intelligence from highest awareness. This "awareness" is the step beyond "consciousness," as consciousness is a man-generated term that causes us to look outside of ourselves for the ability to access our knowing. Awareness utilizes all sensory receptors inside and outside the body to provide a higher perception of what is taking place within our personal field and the group fields within which humans move. All information (vibration) moves within fields. There are many versions of the "field" and we must be aware of which one we are talking about. In order to access the greater field at the highest potential, you must first learn to work within your own personal field and how it is affected from the outside, as well as how what is going on internally affects everything on the outside.

The body is affected by subconscious or hidden beliefs that keep it from being in perfect health and resonating at a higher vibration. For more than a year, I have been praying for my personal merkabah or light-body to be restructured and repaired. I knew I had to let go of whatever thoughts, beliefs, attitudes that were blocking me if I wanted to embody higher aspects of my soul. Boy, did my prayers bring up some crap to deal with! Childhood traumas, relationship issues, social disappointments, emotional pain and grief, illnesses, injuries, and everything else that needed to be released was waiting in line (not so patiently) for its turn to be resolved. During that time, my ego acted demanding, intolerant, critical, whiny, arrogant, and helpless. Shadow-side integration is what 2013 was all about for me and several people I know. The work is done in the template, I assure you, but we have yet to change the routing that keeps us from going back into our old stories. Those stories and the mind, ego, emotions are being shattered by the frequencies of purer consciousness that we are interfacing with. And, the clearing process will only get more intense if we resist it. Still, even at this point, we are all better off not carrying as much energy and repressed emotions from our past.

There are many other realms or fields in the multiverse, including the "primordial soup" that holds the potential or possibility for everything that can be created. Some call it the "nothingness" that contains limitless possibilities for everything. This is the source of infinite creative power. The realm where ascended masters, galactic councils, angelic beings, and other highly-evolved entities of light reside is where the upgrades are being made in the template that affects humanity. We can tune into the template and know what is going on there. It's like listening to the radio. If you can't hear what is being played, you turn up the volume. In other words, adjust the decibel settings or the force of the vibration as it is being released.

One who is allowing the upgrades, engaging them, or working with them will utilize their entire multi-sensory system and continue noticing the subtle signals more and more. Knowing what is occurring in the higher dimension helps us cooperate and can mean the difference between what I call the "whisper" or the "cosmic two-by-four." Those who are still in their heads and not engaging with their higher guidance may get a little "nudge." This is what happened to me last October. My ability to hear, see, sense, and smell in the spirit realm greatly increased after my head injury. That story is in the next chapter.

A New Way to Connect

For centuries, we have used brain-to-brain connection with one another through our logic and intellect. Template upgrades in recent decades have allowed us to move from a database of information previously accepted as truth to a place of "knowing from the heart" in a more loving and accepting way. We have been connecting heart to heart, and we feel the warmth of that connection. However, those upgrades left us with some gaps in communication that created confusion within our soul's interface with our guidance team. Another upgrade was necessary for a resonant field to be created that allows us to communicate using our "heart-mind" and the wisdom of our highest expression of soul, which is now being housed more fully within the body. This recent upgrade or molecular restructuring has to do with our being able to sustain "form" while moving into higher dimensions and remaining a resident upon the planet. While multifaceted upgrades have been completed and are ready to positively affect humanity, the human body has not caught up with the process that will allow more awareness and higher aspects of the soul to be housed in the body. We need more resonance among humans in order to facilitate the shift into our light-body without chaos. One way this resonance can be achieved is through light language that connects us to the advanced intelligence of our higher selves and guidance team.

In addition to upgrades within the molecular structure, the encoding within the DNA and cellular matrix has been given additional codes that allowed us to recognize telepathic exchanges within our group field. This caused many people to become extremely empathic over the past decade. Many are able to sense, and even experience, the thoughts, feelings, and energy of people, animals, plants, and non-bodied beings. This upgrade also activated light language in many people. Light language is the soul's expression of its direct divine connection with Source. It can be written, spoken, sung, drawn, danced, and conveyed in many ways.

At first glance and experience, spoken light language sounds like gibberish, but upon closer observation, you will notice that often the person who is hearing it seems to recognize it. Some people have begun hearing a mysterious dialog or language forming in their thoughts. Whenever you hear light language in your mind it is important to open your mouth and give form to it, no matter how strange it might sound. You might do this in a private environment to begin with. The more you are willing to experience light language, the more "normal" it becomes and you might soon find that you, and others, recognize something that can't be explained. This vibrational exchange is activating the cellular and DNA encoding from the upgrade and is assisting in the expression of our higher selves in the body as well as on the planet. More positive changes are coming and light language can help bring them online.

If a higher aspect of your multidimensional soul visits the Earth body and finds it ready to receive and hold the vibration it carries, it will integrate peacefully with other aspects already in the body. (We will talk about hearing the voices of these aspects in a later chapter.) We have to engage with the shadow aspects of our souls as well so we are no longer going through the motions of just surviving from one day to the next. We must embrace and truly hear the voices of our soul aspects if we want to start "being" rather than just "doing" life. Looking fully into the mirrors of our shadow side will remove fear, lack, limitations, and beliefs that prevent us from anchoring the vibration of our higher selves. This does not mean we have to re-live trauma—that only takes us back into the old emotional energy and reinforces the negative experience. Instead, we acknowledge the shadow aspect, have a dialog with it, thank it for its service, and help it feel safe enough to come into the light.

If the body is not ready to hold a higher vibration, it will activate a clearing and recalibrating to move out old energy and thought patterns that are preventing the body from shifting its structure. Have you had a dark night of the soul or periods in which you integrated the shadow side or lesser evolved aspects of your soul? I had to get knocked in the head in order to move out of a pattern of negativity. I was resistant and stuck; I could not clear it through the affirmations, brainwave entrainment audios, hypnosis CDs, prayers, energy work, or other methods I have used and taught in my previous books. I am thankful for this intervention, even though it was painful to endure. It sidelined me, kept me in bed for weeks, and tested my patience as I learned to surrender and flow in an unpleasant situation. It was while I laid in bed resting because it hurt too much to be up and mobile that I received downloads of information and felt angels and other beings of light ministering to my body, mind, and emotions. This is when light language reactivated and began changing my life.

As I go about my slower-paced daily life now, the annoying mental chatter that I used to experience is significantly less; I am more peaceful, I feel energy flowing most of the time, my inner guidance is clearer, and I'm less concerned about having what I need. I say this to encourage you if you are going through a difficult time that seems to be never-ending and serving no purpose. The Universe makes no mistakes. You are on an ascension journey and whatever you are experiencing is simply part of the plan.

Light language is a very powerful ascension tool that allows us to communicate soul to soul with our guidance team, as well as with one another. It can be used for self-healing, merkabah restoration, light-body activation, inter-dimensional travel, manifestation of material resources, and directing energy. I believe this loving ancient language of light and vibration can open our "junk" DNA, thus reconnecting us with our original blueprint that some refer to as Adam Kadmon.

Brain Waves

Our brain pulses and vibrates like everything else in the world. You have probably heard of a machine called an EEG or electroencephalograph, which is used to measure brain pulse. Brain pulsations are measured in cycles per second, or hertz. Through the course of a day, the brain can enter various states of awareness: beta, alpha, theta, and delta.

- Beta (13- 40 cycles per second) is our predominant state during daily activity.
- Alpha (8-13 cycles per second) is a state of wakefulness with relaxed alertness. You may reach this state while in light meditation or daydreaming.
- Theta (4-7 cycles per second) is the state we reach during creativity, deep meditation, or in the dream state. This is where our extra-sensory perception

(ESP) operates best and why we see deceased loved ones while dreaming.

- Delta (1/2 - 4 cycles per second) is the state of deep sleep. This very slow vibrating pattern is conducive to astral projection or out-of-body experiences.

Brainwave audios use sound waves, pulses, and binaural beats to alter the vibration and draw the brain into altered states of consciousness. Hypnosis uses the power of suggestion to affect the subconscious mind and help a person make changes in thoughts, habits, and behavior. Repeating affirmations can also have a positive benefit. Meditation is also a good tool for quieting the mind and finding peace. Deep breathing can help the body calm down and heal itself. But, none of these affect our reality and physical health as much, as fast, or as permanently as we would like for them to. That's because the subconscious thoughts, beliefs, and programming rule about 95 percent of our body's functions and life experiences. Our subconscious minds are stronger than our conscious thoughts and beliefs; so, when we say we want to be healed and we have a subconscious belief that we deserve to suffer, guess which is going to have the most impact? These self-limiting programs running in the background of our minds have an effect upon everything in our lives. If we are to reprogram damaging thought patterns in the subconscious mind, we must tap into the DNA upgrades I mentioned above.

The brain is not the mind. The brain dies with the body and does not go with us into the afterlife. The mind is the mental/emotional recorder and playback system of the DNA. The mind and the electromagnetic imprint of our DNA goes with us into the afterlife as part of the Akashic record for our soul's journey. Soul evolution continues in an array of dimensions and realities in the afterlife. When we reincarnate, the DNA that holds our personal multi-life histories and experiences comes back with us in order for the soul to continue the process of development into an ascended state that eventually no longer needs to reincarnate.

According to Rudolph E. Tanzi, Ph.D., the author of *Super Brain*, "The wiring of your brain is constantly changing, depending on your thoughts, feelings, beliefs, and habits." Since the brain is forever changing—not always for the better—how do we change our subconscious beliefs so we can heal our bodies, make positive changes, and find peace of mind? It can begin by altering your DNA through light language, which is not affected by the subconscious, the brain, or the body, but rather by our higher selves and Source energy. Unless light language is interpreted, the logical brain cannot understand what is being said or conveyed. While some people discredit the practice of speaking this "unknown" idiom that many times simply cannot be deciphered, it is for that very reason that it is so effective.

Altering DNA through Light Language

The original discovery of DNA showed our genes were fixed and unchanging, and that they controlled our physical appearance, behavior, and predisposition to disease. However, more recent studies show that our environment, personal preferences, thoughts, emotions, words, actions, decisions, lifestyles, and beliefs have an influence upon our DNA. Therefore, we can evolve our DNA through our choices!

The body has the ability to reset and heal itself on an ongoing basis. From the time we are babies, we are programmed to believe that our body is supposed to get sick, and that the doctor and pharmaceuticals are the only methods for healing. This is contrary to the divine programming that is possible to unlock in the human body. The human body can and should be the authority for healing itself. I believe changes to our DNA can be made by the activation of light codes contained in our DNA. Codes are transmitted through light language that can override and reprogram old beliefs and patterns that keep the body sick and in disrepair.

Dr. Suzan Caroll states the following about light language and DNA:

> *Because Light Language is the language of your multidimensional self, downloading this language and integrating it into your body greatly expands your consciousness and frees you from the confines of linear, logical thinking. As your consciousness expands into multidimensional thinking, you can receive and understand messages from higher and higher frequencies of light, as well as messages from the quantum realities and "dark matter." It is the Light of these multidimensional messages that "turns on" your "junk DNA" and begins the process of returning to SELF, even while you are still living within a physical form.* [1]

Kelly Beavers senses shapes, colors, and numbers accompanied by images in the auras and heart spaces of people with whom she interacts. She believes these are codes intended to allow human DNA to evolve and to support various creations on Earth. She has had experiences in meditation that involve math and numbers in a multidimensional way. Kelly has a master's degree and four years toward her PhD in urban planning. Lately, she has been receiving codes when communicating with people and she senses her future purpose will incorporate her shamanic awareness with urban planning. When she looks at proposed plans for trains, bus systems, and other transportation systems, the information is deeply layered with energetic information.

We humans are not alone on this planet. Starseeds are among us in human bodies; some are hybrids, which means they have part human DNA and part extra-terrestrial DNA. We also have off-planet support surrounding the earth. They are making their presence known to us in non-threatening ways. Crop circles are galactic signs or compressed codes that are helping us to anchor the grid for the New Earth and unlock the codes in human DNA that will bring about the new superhuman that Mary Rodwell talks about. In addition to being the co-founder and principal of ACERN (Australian Close Encounter Resource Network) Mary Rodwell is an RN, midwife, counselor, hypnotherapist, and metaphysician. The primary focus of her work is supporting people who have had contact with advanced extraterrestrial intelligences. Mary has obtained over 1,600 testimonies that show how our galactic counterparts are preparing us to accept their presence on our planet (http://tinyurl.com/mjfz6uu).

Chapter 2 ~ There Are No Accidents . . . Right?

I didn't know shopping was an impact sport until I made an embarrassing scene at the Atlanta IKEA one Saturday night in October. I released four packages (weighing about eight pounds each) of 118-inch long canvas draperies with a thud onto a hand truck, and the metal handle flipped up and hit me in the forehead. Hard! Think of stepping on a rake and the handle flying up and you will get the picture. It smacked me in the forehead so hard that it caused my glasses to cut into my face. My neck was snapped backward beyond its natural curve, resulting in a mammoth whiplash. I was so stunned that I felt my knees buckling and voluntarily sat down on the concrete floor before risking a second injury should I pass out, which my mother was not going to allow. She warned me not to scare her by doing such a dramatic thing. I mean, come on! Blunt force trauma to the forehead is not an excuse to lose consciousness! I am so glad she was with me; it would have been dangerous for me to drive in this condition. I was unable to think straight or get my words to come out as fast as I wanted them to.

The store called someone to bring a first aid kit and some ice. The attendant filled out an accident report because that's what they do when someone leaves a blood sample in the store. However, I wasn't about to leave my bargain drapes behind. It was my excitement over finding such a deal on cabana curtains for my new back porch that caused me to become careless enough to create this injury. I would, by god, take home a trophy. So, after we decided that I didn't need stitches, I was escorted in a wheelchair to a private checkout lane. Even though we used the secret employee corridors, I did *not* get an employee discount. I did get to keep the bloody dish towel as a souvenir.

The next morning, I looked like the beast in Beauty and the Beast. The Y-shaped cut between my eyes was superglued shut with Liquid Bandage and butterfly tape. We had no idea how serious the injury really was—especially since I had managed to drive the five hours home that day. But, by Monday evening I was feeling horrible, having terrible mood swings, a monster headache, and was totally exhausted. And, that was just the beginning.

I experienced a great deal of pain and stayed close to home for months after the accident because being in social settings was over-stimulating. I was not only dealing with brain trauma, which manifested as extreme sensitivity to sound and light, my body was having symptoms of PTSD (post-traumatic stress disorder). I could no longer handle stress of any kind, which meant driving was an extremely difficult task, and I could not predict my need for rest while my sleeping patterns were so sporadic. I was saddened when I had to stop babysitting my four-year-old grandson. I had enjoyed spending time with him every week since he was a baby. Every time I felt better and pushed to return to normal life, I would have a setback and end up in bed for days afterward in order to recuperate. It was two steps forward and one step backward. I dictated much of this book into a voice-to-text program, many times while lying in bed with a heating pad on my aching neck, back, and shoulders. During my down time, I drew inward and began to really listen to all those voices in my head: my inner child, my critical parent, my guides and soul group members, other aspects of my soul, my body, and even my ego as it expressed its fears and unresolved issues that needed to be dealt with.

I went to my holistic medical doctor, who recommended supplements for balancing and supporting brain chemicals that were out of whack due to stress/trauma. He said I likely still had some swelling around the brain so he put me on a supplement for inflammation. Then, a natural sleep aid to help restore healthy sleep patterns, and something to detox my liver from all the Tylenol and pain killers I had been taking. After draining my bank account and taking two doses of this conglomeration, I started feeling like a human (instead of road kill) again.

In the months preceding the IKEA incident, I had asked why at least 100 times. *Why* do I not know what I'm supposed to do next? Everyone in my women's circle seemed to be getting guidance and new opportunities were opening for them. I felt stagnant. *Why* do I not smell that fragrance I used to smell when I was younger? *Why* have I become so negative? The Universe definitely has a sense of humor. The injury site on my forehead had a cut in the shape of the letter "Y." The question I asked most was *why* did I stop remembering my dreams or seeing day visions after my walk-in in 1999? One day in late summer, I finally heard an answer: "She slammed the door." *What door? She who?* I thought it meant that LavendarRose had shut the door to the dream world when she walked in.

As I wrestled with my recovery that first month, I rephrased my questions and left out the word "why." Instead, I asked, "Is it normal for it to take so long to recover from a whiplash? Is there anything I can do to speed up the healing process? Is there something I need to learn or discover in this situation? Did I smack my head to get my third eye to open so I could have dreams and visions again? What is the purpose of this pain and suffering? I got small messages like "see a chiropractor," or "get a massage," or "stay in bed and rest," or "get myofascial release therapy."

The discomfort I was having between my shoulder blades was the same place I had experienced fibromyalgia after my 1999 soul exchange. There seemed to be a correlation. Had I experienced another soul exchange? It sure seemed like something was different, but I had had a traumatic brain injury and everything in my body was out of kilter. How would I even know if I had a different soul?

The message "she slammed the door," made sense the morning I awoke knowing LavendarRose had left and there was a new soul in my body. Things changed drastically after that and my guidance became clearer than it had ever been prior. I felt confused and disoriented much of that day—I could not remember what decade it was! When I heard my guides say that this walk-in was a year late coming into the body, I knew it was LavendarRose who "slammed the door" in 2011 and said no to the walk-in when 76-99 came back to pick up where she had left off on her mission. A lot of things started making sense. It became apparent that LavendarRose had been a placeholder soul who did not have access to the dream state where many of my mission instructions are given. While she had done a fabulous job of caring for the body and holding the reins of the mission she did not fully understand, she had also become attached to Earth life and did not want to give up the body. After I realized I had experienced a soul exchange, pieces of the puzzle fell into place, and in less than a month I had started writing this book.

> *Opening soon will be much new knowledge within the language of light. Light will replace completely the written word in a few short years of Earth time.*
> *~ Snow Eagle Seeds Sing*

During the third week of writing this book, I had an opportunity to attend a dream weaver seminar. The night before the actual event started, I went to a friend's house where I met a healer named Vic, who felt led to do galactic surgery on me to help move trauma out of the cells of my body. Before I arrived, Vic drew a card with me in mind. The card from Dianna 'Snow Eagle Seeds Sing' Henry's oracle deck, *Spirit of Corn Maize Wisdom Cards* read: "Opening soon will be much new knowledge within the language of light. Light will replace completely the written word in a few short years of Earth time." The session with Vic went well and my body (as well as my emotions) felt peaceful for the first time in months.

It was not surprising that the dream weaver weekend not only activated my dreams and visions that had been "offline" for more than a decade, but also activated light language for other attendees. I can't even begin to explain what it was like to be submerged in light language, prophecy, drumming, and the vibration of singing for almost forty-eight hours. My life was positively changed and my ministry was activated in a way like I have never experienced. Miracles are a part of my daily life now.

Mother Mary came in strong that weekend. We built an altar before we started the opening circle on Friday night, and someone put a Black Madonna statue in the center. The Madonna (representative of Mother Sophia) had been broken some time ago and glued back together. The shape of her "wound" matched the shape of mine. I could hear Bill Engvall, saying, "Here's your sign." My hunch is that the incident at IKEA opened a portal for Mother Sophia to heal the earth and humanity through me. I am one of countless many who are here for this purpose.

You are likely sensing huge changes in your soul's expression on Earth. If you sense that you have had an actual soul exchange, you may want to read *Walk-ins Among Us* or visit WalkinsAmongUs.org.

Synchronicity abounds as you learn to recognize the voice of your higher guidance and interpret the meanings. Light language can help to open your understanding regarding what is happening for you personally. This unsolicited phenomenon is emerging to assist you as you ascend into higher consciousness. Your soul aspects and fragments are coming home, and you may be hearing the voices of those many aspects. They can actually assist you on this journey.

In the next chapter, we will explore how light language began showing up in charismatic spirit-filled churches in recent decades, and how it is now emerging in the everyday lives of ordinary people like you and me.

Chapter 3 ~ Speaking in Tongues? No Way, José!

Light language is not a new phenomenon. According to Chief Golden Light Eagle, these languages have been used throughout the centuries by indigenous people to connect with their star system and galactic families.

The Bible mentions light language, calling it the gift of tongues in I Corinthians 12: 10.

> *He gives power for doing miracles to some, and to others power to prophesy and preach. He gives someone else the power to know whether evil spirits are speaking through those who claim to be giving God's messages—or whether it is really the Spirit of God who is speaking. Still another person is able to speak in languages he never learned; and others, who do not know the language either, are given power to understand what he is saying.*

Jesus attempted to bring this language of light back online more than 2,000 years ago when he promised to send the "comforter" or an advocate to take his place after he ascended. His ministry attempted to demonstrate the divinity of humans. I sense that the ability to speak or write a language you could not have acquired by natural means (xenoglossy), which occurred on the Day of Pentecost, was a reactivation of cosmic language. I believe that the gift of tongues (light language) is still available today. Jesus is recorded as having said, "Anything I can do, you can do, and more."

On the Day of Pentecost, the ability to understand and speak in unlearned languages was demonstrated. Everyone assembled in the upper room heard and understood what was being said as if it had been spoken in their native languages. Acts 2 tells the story of what happened:

> *When the day of Pentecost came, they were all together in one place. Suddenly a sound like the blowing of a violent wind came from Heaven and filled the whole house where they were sitting. They saw what seemed to be tongues of fire that separated and came to rest on each of them. All of them were filled with the Holy Spirit and began to speak in other tongues as the Spirit enabled them. Now there were staying in Jerusalem God-fearing Jews from every nation under Heaven. When they heard this sound, a crowd came together in bewilderment, because each one heard their own language being spoken. Utterly amazed, they asked: "Aren't all these who are speaking Galileans? Then how is it that each of us hears them in our native language? Parthians, Medes and Elamites; residents of Mesopotamia, Judea and Cappadocia, Pontus and Asia, Phrygia and Pamphylia, Egypt and the parts of Libya near Cyrene; visitors from Rome (both Jews and converts to Judaism); Cretans and Arabs—we hear*

them declaring the wonders of God in our own tongues!" Amazed and perplexed, they asked one another, "What does this mean?" Some, however, made fun of them and said, "They have had too much wine."

Too much wine? I'm not sure what you are thinking, but just speaking another language would probably not create enough stir to bring the neighbors over, much less to have them think the people speaking these languages were drunk. There must have been some peculiar behavior or manifestations accompanying the download! Later on in this book, I will offer insight about what might have happened by giving some modern-day examples and my own experiences with this "wine" of the spirit. I wonder what my neighbors think of the drumming, chanting, singing, and strange languages they hear coming from my back porch and yard. In the past, I participated in prophetic meetings where those who were not on the "spirit medication" thought we were absolutely crazy. Yet, they saw the power and positive effects produced by our "birthing in the spirit." In those gatherings, I experienced healing and shifts in consciousness when others spoke light language to me. I have witnessed similar responses in others when light language was spoken on their behalf. Recently, a friend had a qigong session right after we had spoken light language with one another. Four guardians from Orion came into that session. She felt like their presence was a direct result of heightening her experience with light language through our interaction.

This language of the soul is also known as galactic language, star language, or angel language, as well as praying, speaking, or uttering in unknown tongues. This latter term, however, has a stigma attached to it due to religions that have demonstrated the practice in such a bizarre and fantastical fashion. The ability to communicate with Source and not have interference of the logical mind can be very helpful. However, many people in Western society have had an unpleasant encounter with the phenomena known as speaking in tongues. As a result, they have a bad *taste* (pun intended) in their mouths because of it. Therefore, a public setting might not be the best place to demonstrate this ability unless those in attendance have some basic knowledge about what light language is. The Bible suggests that there be an interpreter present in order for glossolalia (the vocalizing of speech-like syllables that lack any readily comprehended meaning) to be helpful to a group of people. I don't think an interpretation is necessary or even useful at times. It is meant to override the conditioning and programming of the logical mind and allow one to commune directly with Source. However, if you are in a lecture-type meeting and someone erupts into ecstatic babbling without warning, it could rattle a few cages. Some may wonder if the outburst will be followed by someone pulling a poisonous snake out of a bag. This actually happened in a church service my ex-husband attended as a child.

Regardless of this gift's tainted modern-day history, I thank my Pentecostal and Charismatic Christian brothers and sisters for bringing this tool, this resource, to my attention.

After my near-death experience in 1976, I became curious about the gifts of the spirit listed in I Corinthians 12 and had been praying to receive all nine gifts. By the early 1990s, I had evidenced all of the gifts except for the ability to speak in tongues. And, I wasn't sure if I had the ability to interpret them since I had not heard people speak in an unknown tongue, even though I was attending a Pentecostal Church of God whose denominational headquarters are in Cleveland, Tennessee. One day in 1994, Kathy, my prayer partner, came over for our regular prayer time. She was excited that she had received the gift of praying in tongues. Inwardly, I felt jealous, but I was too shy to try her suggestion to receive the gift by simply starting to make vowel sounds and allowing the language to bubble up. It could *not* be that easy. *Could* it?

After Kathy left, curiosity got the best of me. I went to my bedroom and closed the door so my kids couldn't hear me. Very timidly, I began to intone and move my lips asking that the Holy Spirit, whom I now recognize as the Divine Mother, to help me "stir up" this ability and bring it forth as a prayer tool. After a minute or so, I spoke a few syllables that sounded like "porta-reek-may-co-con-tay-go." Hmmm . . . Was I going to be a missionary in Puerto Rico? At the time, I had no concept that conscious life forms existed anywhere except on our planet; therefore, I just *knew* I had spoken an Earth language that could be verified by someone who spoke it. I phonetically wrote down the phrase and for years shared it with bilingual people I came in contact with. No one could give me an interpretation. While writing this article I asked my guidance what the phrase means and heard "You have asked and received." Cool!

Throughout the rest of the day I kept repeating the mystery phrase. Other utterances came as well, but nothing as clear as the first phrase so I didn't write anything down or try to remember what I had spoken. The next day I wondered if I had imagined the whole thing and if the ability would still be there. It was! And, I spoke it throughout that day, and the next, and the next, and for years thereafter. Seems so simple that anyone could do it. Maybe by the time you finish reading this book, you would consider giving it a try—or *another* try if you have already done this in the past.

> *Ephesians 5:19: "Speaking to yourselves in psalms and hymns and spiritual songs, singing and making melody in your heart to the Lord."*

Emily Singleton has always been a skeptic about speaking in tongues. In her younger years, she believed it to be a sensationalized act that could not possibly be an authentic experience. She made fun of it and the people who claimed to engage in it. When she got older, her uncle began to speak in tongues. She had never personally witnessed him speak it, but she trusted him. So, she had to re-evaluate her perceptions. It came as a shock to her when she had an experience in her own life that some might call speaking in tongues. As far as speaking in tongues in the religious community, Emily has seen people use unknown languages for good, and some not so good. She says, "It has been used for darker purposes too many times for the purity of its impact to be trusted." This is her observation and not meant to be a judgment against the church.

Maybe you've had a bad experience with the church and its system. Now that you have left organized religion, anything that slightly resembles those practices repulses you. I rode that angry horse for years before I came to peace in owning my truth. Allowing a past experience to stop you from employing a useful tool is like throwing the baby out with the bath water. The language I got privately at home sounds the same as one of the dialects I still speak. Perhaps reading this book will help you see the benefits of speaking light language.

Randall Hawk's experience with light language came while attending a charismatic church that was part of the Vineyard Association. He pressed the pause button on his expression when he became disgruntled with the church and left organized religion in 2001. He reactivated it in 2014 and has used it for healing himself and others. So, as you can see from this and other examples I have mentioned, you do *not* lose when you snooze.

Why Is Light Language Emerging Now?

Ever since December 21, 2012, we have seen an increase in spiritual/psychic gifts. This is likely because more starseeds have come to live on the planet, both as born-in star children and as walk-ins. The upgrades made in the human template are coming on line and activating the codes in dormant DNA strands. The language of light also seems to be contagious! It is activated by hearing it; the more who hear it, the more who will speak, write, sing, draw, and sign it.

Another reason for light language to emerge now is because we are at the end of the precessional cycle that takes approximately 26,000 years to complete. This period of time is referred to as the "last days." What we see happening with the reemergence of light language today is the return of Christ consciousness, which was prophesied in the Old Testament as well as in Acts 2: 17.

In the last days, God says, "I will pour out my Spirit on all people. Your sons and daughters will prophesy, your young men will see visions, your old men will dream dreams. Even on my servants, both men and women, I will pour out my Spirit in those days, and they will prophesy."

Enoch was a priest-scientist who lived before the Great Flood. He is associated with the building of the Great Pyramid complex. In the Bible, he was the father of Methuselah and great-grandfather of Noah. Enoch is known to the Egyptians as Thoth, and to the Greeks as Hermes, and in the Celtic tradition as Merlin the Wizard. In all these cultures and traditions, even the Mayan legend of Quetzacoatal, Enoch promises a return of his knowledge at "the end of time" or our current time cycle. The Book of Enoch, originally composed in Hebrew, was considered an authoritative scripture by early Christians and was widely read and used during the first three centuries after the death of Christ. In 381 AD, the Council of Laodicia discredited and banned the scripture. Parts of the Book of Enoch, written in Aramaic, were discovered in the Dead Sea Scrolls.

In his book, *The Keys of Enoch*, written in 1973, Dr. J.J. Hurtak refers to a "language of light" or mother tongue. This language, known as Hiburu, is said to be the seed language of a pre-flood civilization known as Atlantis. The Keys of Enoch are sonic equations or sacred geometry encoded within the ancient mantras. By intoning specific ancient sounds, a scientific team was able to produce visible standing waves of light above and within the pyramids. And, they were able to penetrate chambers that were previously inaccessible. The Keys of Enoch are also capable of directly affecting the brain and nervous system, thereby producing healing and higher states of consciousness. While the light language we speak may not be the literal Keys of Enoch, they contain vibrations and light that connect us with Source. All of these scientific findings, our rapidly changing life experiences, and archeological discoveries prove that we truly are undergoing a transformation process that many refer to as the ascension.

A Unified World Language

Perhaps light language is the universal language spoken on Earth prior to the Tower of Babel. This account is mentioned in the eleventh chapter of the book of Genesis in the Christian Bible. This seems to have occurred shortly after the Great Flood, which as Barbara Hand Clow documented in her book, *Awakening the Planetary Mind*, was about 11,500 years ago.

> *Now the whole world had one language and a common speech. As people moved eastward, they found a plain in Shinar and settled there. They said to each other, "Come, let's make bricks and bake them thoroughly." They used brick instead of stone, and tar for mortar. Then they said, "Come, let us build ourselves a city, with a tower that reaches to the Heavens, so that we may make a name for ourselves; otherwise we will be scattered over the face of the whole Earth." But the Lord [possibly Nephilim or other cosmic beings with harmful intentions] came down to see the city and the tower the people were building. The Lord said, "If as one people speaking the same language they have begun to do this, then nothing they plan to do will be impossible for them. Come, let us go down and confuse their language so they will not understand*

each other." So the Lord scattered them from there over all the Earth, and they stopped building the city. That is why it was called Babel—because there the Lord confused the language of the whole world. From there the Lord scattered them over the face of the whole Earth.

If ill-intending cosmic beings considered humans having a unified language so "dangerous" that they needed to stop them, then perhaps you can see how important it is for us to speak this cosmic language once again.

The emergence of light language in the past century came about in ways that caused many people to question the validity of this tool as it appeared in charismatic and Pentecostal churches in the US. Some have sensationalized "tongues" and caused many to disdain the practice. I believe there are many "closet" light language speakers who once used this gift and would like to reactivate and use it to help humanity heal and ascend. Thank you for being willing to go with me on this exploration. Perhaps, like me, you will find that it is quite fun to express your creative nature by speaking, singing, intoning, writing, dancing, and signing in this beautiful language of light.

Chapter 4 ~ The Purpose of Light Language

You can speak light language anytime to the Creator, yourself, your pets, your children, your guides and angels, your plants, other people, the Earth, inanimate objects, upcoming or current situations, etc. It comes in handy when you are in crisis or when you simply want to keep yourself company while driving. It is a great way to distract the mind from "going places" you would rather not go.

We are fully responsible for all our creations—even the stuff that happens when we are creating by default through our underlying beliefs, thoughts, and patterns. Because it is spirit-to-spirit communication with our Creator, light language can reveal and transform ingrained patterns in our subconscious. Even though we are not always intellectually aware of what we are communicating through light language, we are consciously creating a new reality when we set our intention to apply light to a thought or situation. Light language is a very powerful healing modality and a tool for change.

Try this: make a prayer list of things you would like to "treat" with light language. Notice your body, thoughts, and emotions. Begin speaking, drawing, dancing, signing, or writing in light language. Go for at least five minutes or until you sense a shift. Again, notice your body, thoughts, and emotions. What is different? Do you have a sense of what transpired? Many times you will get an idea of what you have healed or transmuted in yourself or another person or situation simply by the way the energy shifts while you are intentionally using light language. Because light knows what to do, your light language treatment may touch and heal something in another lifetime or soul aspect. When that aspect heals, you will feel it present tense.

Maryanne Savino began speaking light language about ten years ago after being activated by two friends, Jodi Serota and Judy Satori. She feels that her first experience with light languages awakened codes of light that had been dormant in her DNA for many lifetimes. Now, when she is speaking light language, she can sometimes translate the message, but most of the time it is about bypassing the ego mind and just allowing the vibrational energy to flow through and be felt. Maryanne believes light language serves various purposes. It raises vibration and expands consciousness, assists with clearing negative imprints from past life issues, releases limiting beliefs systems and negative patterns and programming, aligns a person with their divine purpose, and assists with the ascension journey. "As we continue to shift with Mother Earth it [light language] can ease ascension symptoms and open us to our unique creative gifts and abilities," said Maryanne. "Angels, star/galactic beings and Earth spirits sing through her. These are what she calls Divine Mother sacred transmissions."

The energy that is transmitted through light language can be intense, depending on the speaker. Yet it is also fun because, like any artistic endeavor, it is the energy of creation. I love to speak it and hear it spoken as I did during a two-day workshop in which we spoke in light language as much as we did in English! One woman chose to only speak in light language accompanied by signing in light language (intuitive hand mudras), and by drawing pictures or words. During one of the sessions, the group telepathically communicated with light language and drew a geometric representation of what the woman who only spoke light language was seeing. That drawing gave us messages about what our dream weaving was doing for the Earth and collective humanity. While the entire experience was fun and exciting, it had a higher purpose. My life was changed from the experiences I had that weekend.

I have personally been using languages of light since 1994 and I have seen positive results from the practice. I let the habit fall to the wayside for many years. Since I started speaking light language everyday (for hours if you include what I'm hearing internally) since December 2013, my body has healed from the trauma of the head injury and whiplash. More progress was made during the first week that I was writing this book and speaking light language than was made in the previous two months. That is enough proof of its effectiveness for me, but there are many more ways that light language can help you on your journey toward wholeness.

Spiritual Transformation

Light language helps us to connect with the still small voice within, which gives us reliable guidance on real day-to-day decisions. Regular use with the right intentions accelerates our spiritual growth and self-mastery. Because it carries codes, it helps to open our mind by activating our psychological, neurological, and biochemical levels and attune to higher thoughts. Light language must be raising my vibration. A woman in my yoga class touched my foot one day and said her whole body started vibrating. That was the second time since I started speaking light language on a daily basis that someone told me their body vibrated after having contact with my body.

A friend of mine activated light language not too long ago. Soon after, she had a beautiful spiritual encounter in which she went to the void and beyond, to where all energy comes from. She said, "There is no light as we know it here—only purity of Source. It felt even deeper than the heart of God energy! No words can describe the lightness of being. No body, no thoughts. Just BE-ing." This brought deeper visions, more inter-connections about her path from here forward and much healing about where she had been. She said she felt like the rest of her deepest soul has come home from long before the earth was ever even formed.

Eliminating Detrimental Thoughts

In the past, I have tried to be careful not to judge anyone or allow degrading thoughts to stay in my mind. I have tried to stay in the now moment and focus on what is good about a person or situation. If I caught myself starting to criticize, I would imagine a road-block and see myself going the opposite way. However, my monkey mind has a four-wheel drive and can find detours that lead right back to any road-block I set up. That girl can plow through a visualized blockade, go down a detrimental path, and spin mud all over the place before I realize what's happening. After my walk-in on November 23, I felt wonderfully different. I wanted to stay in that state of bliss so I asked my guidance how I might avoid falling back into the ruts of unhealthy ingrained patterns. My guidance, which has become much clearer since November 2013, said that my neural pathways had been cleared like a tooth that has had a root canal. I could relate to that because I had just spent $1,330 having that painful experience. Like the roots of my tooth that were filled in with a material that would allow it to be strong and function without pain, the ruts in my neural pathways were being filled in with "light" material. I now know my guides were speaking of the upgrades that are activated by light language. Speaking light language has worked incredibly well to calm my monkey mind.

A couple of weeks after receiving these instructions, I awoke from having a dream in which I felt like I was being held down by something invisible. This same thing happened again about a week later. I had not had this kind of dreamlike paralysis and fear since the mid-1990s when I was doing spiritual warfare and battling dark entities. Actually, only *part* of me felt fearful. The higher soul aspect observing this situation felt neutral and unmoved by it. As I lay there awake, I heard my guidance say that this was not happening currently, but that more of my neural pathways were being cleared of traumatic experiences I had had in this life and in past lives. I started speaking light language as I laid there. The fearful feeling completely left within a minute.

Our thoughts separate us because they have been programmed to put out dissonant vibrations that are contrary to oneness. Light language is useful when you need to shift a situation or resolve conflict with someone (or within yourself). It is a great tool to help bring something into harmony with the highest and best solution. If you have "temptations" arising from what you consider to be your ego, you may want to consider that one of your shadow aspects is bringing up something to be integrated. Use light language to treat it with a vibration that can bring it into resonation with the higher aspects.

Healing Self and Others

Light language can create healing for you and others.

Terri DeMarco says, "The language of light comes to us on the waves of sound, through symbolism, crystalline frequencies, and light. It is the divine equations, sacred ratios, sacred geometry, and resonate frequencies that form the building blocks of all of life . . . the gift of higher dimensional frequency healing." [1]

Veronica O'Grady uses light language during client sessions and says that the intricacies of the codes and geometries they contain are beyond brilliant. And what downloads into people with these songs creates such big shifts for them. She says that light languages are "putting sound to geometries, and bringing geometries through with sound." There's no way she would hold back something that could help her clients, even though she feels self-conscious about expressing this language. Her hesitation in using the codes for herself comes from her experience when she attended an Assemblies of God church that encouraged speaking in tongues. As she looked at people and their energy, she realized they were just doing what they thought they were supposed to do, and it was all fake. They felt so lost.

So, when she sings in the codes for herself, especially if anyone is home, the self-judgment sneaks out. She does not want to sound like an aerie-faerie loon, singing "gibberish" in the way those "speaking in tongues" sounded long ago. My interviewing her for this piece brought up issues around being heard and judged, and judging others. The toning/light language is not the end-all; nor is it a "look at me" kind of thing as she has seen so often. It is just one of the tools in our tool chest—one step in a many-tiered process of healing.

Part of my mission is to activate people into living their authentic selves. So when Veronica told me about the things that have come up for her since seeing my Facebook post about light languages, I was not surprised—one woman started dreaming in light language after we interacted! Veronica was deeply joyful and grateful for the triggering of this inner quest to learn more about these codes that she had been seeing and working with for so long, and to have a chance to heal/dissipate and move beyond her past experiences as she healed her own powerful "voice." So as she ventures forth and puts her voice out there, she will stay tuned to her inner guidance to help her see clearly when the languages are for real and when they are more for show. All the while respecting another person's boldness or freedom in the process. It is a step of trust for anyone venturing out in their own way with this tool. Most are truly coming from the deep place of connection within.

Jess Bray was raised in a Baptist church that did not accept the gifts she brought with her when she was born as a starseed or star traveler in an infant body. It was after meeting Ayesha Nur that she began to reopen the psychic abilities and healing gifts that laid dormant in her DNA. Over the past eight to ten years, she began to discover more of her true self and awaken to her mission as part of a galactic council to assist with transformation. Connecting with her twin flame, who is now her husband, she began remembering her divinity and expanding her daily experience to accept these gifts, which include singing, dancing, and healing the waters through vibration/intonation.

Jess started her healing work about two years ago. During a healing session, she sings and releases vibrational tones over her clients. She started noticing that the syllables she was singing seemed to be a language that she had not consciously learned. While she didn't understand what she was singing, it resonated with her spirit and brought her clients what they needed for personal expansion, so she continued. Today, she speaks many star languages—some of them sound beautiful and gracefully melodic, while others are more tribal, choppy, or guttural. If she is in the energy of another person who is speaking these galactic languages, she understands on a deep soul level (and many times intellectually) what is being communicated. When she and I spoke during a Skype video chat, we both received an intense download of energy that spawned tears of joy at the connection with and remembrance of our starseed origins. I was on a blissful energetic high for two days afterward. This is an indication that we activated codes for one another.

A healer friend of mine wrote me to say she felt like she was getting the "ick" going around. She took Oscillo (for flu), and was going to see her holistic doctor for the Rife Beam Ray Treatment. She says her brain's cells felt like they were hiding out somewhere! I sensed that she was integrating into her physical body some of the DNA upgrades that we are receiving. I encouraged her to let her guides know what is going on and ask them to slow it down just a little bit and then speak to her body about accepting the upgrade.

I got an energy surge when I texted that to her, which usually means confirmation that I'm on the right track. It seemed to me that her brain cells were being activated by these upgrades, so I asked her to speak in her light language over her own body like she does with her clients. I let her know I was sending her a transmission of love and light at that moment so she could intentionally tune into it. Our collaboration produced immediate results. She wrote back a few minutes later in tears of gratitude and recognition: "I had a massive download the other day and told my husband something new was coming in. I forgot about that until reading your words. Profound thank yous, Yvonne. I started with some tones and went to tears big time. Thank you! Wow! And for the beautiful transmission too! So pure!"

Light language not only heals people who are in body here and now, it can go through all portals of time. I was praying in light language in early January 2014 when I suddenly started crying. *Oh, boy,* I thought, *whose stuff have I taken on this time?* Then, I heard that I was clearing the energy of poverty and suffering of my ancestors and healing our family DNA. A re-patterning was occurring in my lineage. I was reminded that when one heals, we all heal. My guidance told me that this clearing would affect not only my ancestors but my descendants as well. All this started from intoning in light language.

Receiving Guidance and Messages from Source

Amenreu Sean grew up in a church that spoke in tongues. During worship, it was not uncommon for people in that church to share a message this way, and there was usually someone who could interpret what had been said. When he was about fourteen years old he was riding in a 17-passenger van on his way to church camp. The kids were playing silly games like truth or dare, which he thought was odd since they were going on a church trip—it seemed disrespectful. So, he suggested they pray instead. Half way through the prayer circle he felt a rush of energy and started speaking in tongues. He was both excited and nervous because he didn't know how his peers would receive this.

He left organized religion a year or two later and started studying eastern philosophies, and got into meditation. He said, "Organized religion cannot depict your spiritual experience. It can influence it, but connection to spirit is innate to each individual. It is our connection to God." He did not use light language again until nearly ten years later when he got a disturbing call from a close friend who had been serving as somewhat of a mentor. The friend said some hurtful things and completely ended the friendship that day. When Sean meditated to find comfort, the light language reactivated and he received his spiritual name, Amenreu. From there, light language moved into a flow of writing that he uses several times a week when journaling.

His light language today sounds the same as it did when it first occurred many years ago, but he rarely speaks it because he isn't comfortable hearing it. The times he does speak it is during ceremonies or when doing energy work through massage that he only offers to close friends. Even then, he uses silent light language to stay centered and focused on following Spirit's direction rather than trying to impose his will for healing or any other outcome onto the person he's massaging. The times when he has spoken it while giving a massage, people have responded by opening their chakras, or energy centers, and said they feel a warm peace that allows them to relax to a greater degree. No one has ever had any adverse reaction to his speaking light language over them. They say it feels familiar.

I've had similar responses with this gift from heaven. Speaking and toning in light language feels like the Galactic Mother's heart tone is coming through me to minister to her children. I described it to a client I was working with as "Mother Sophia (divine feminine energy) singing a lullaby to her baby." And, perhaps our light language sings to Mother as well.

Amenreu hears light language in his head whenever he needs guidance from Spirit. Even then, he doesn't initiate the language, but notices that it is being expressed inwardly. He prays protection over his children and speaks in light language as he puts them to bed at night. Even though he feels a lot of power and buzzes with energy when he speaks it aloud, hearing himself make these vibrations causes his ego to latch onto the situation. That's when he tends to question, "Am I crazy?" or "Is this real?" Yet, he feels certain that the language carries a powerful activation when spoken aloud.

The language is a reflective medium because it calls to light the spirit that we are, and humans aren't used to feeling that grand or light. Amenreu feels energy emanating from the core of his chest or solar plexus when he speaks light language and he is afraid of unleashing this power. He admits that his throat chakra is not as open as the rest of his chakras and he's not ready to fully express his voice.

The first time Emily Singleton became aware of light language was at the Star Knowledge Conference at Serpent Mound, Ohio in 2010. She walked in on a talk that was being given by Amor Luz Pangilinan, who was speaking of light language and the power of sound, light, and vibration to stand in our choices. Amor went into an altered state, and spoke in a galactic tongue. She has been an important presence in Emily's life and in her coming into cosmic awareness. From the first time she saw her, Emily was convinced of Amor's authenticity. She is a very humble person and uses her gifts wisely. Even though Emily did not understand mentally what was being said through Amor, her response was to allow the energy it created to wash over her and soak in.

After that conference, Emily went home and began to have experiences for which she does not have a name. She has heard some people use the term "download," but she is not comfortable using that word to describe what has happened to her personally. As a part of these experiences, her whole body would shake and she would not only see and feel the presence of light, she would actually *become* light, if only for a few seconds. This only happened at night after she had set sacred space alone outside, usually in the hot tub and mostly immersed in water. This allowed her body to become weightless, and she would become aware that she was rising in the water. As soon as her physical being realized this, she would freak out a bit, and it would stop.

Before any of this began, she had been hearing a very high-pitched tone that was only audible in her left ear. It was literally as if a radio was being held to her left ear and the volume turned up, while there was nothing in her right ear. This happened sporadically with no apparent rhyme or reason, but it usually preceded the hot tub light experiences. As a result of these episodes, she felt a calling to record a tuning fork project, which she did from January to December of 2011 (*Frequencies from the Red Star of Orion*). As a part of that project, phrases came into her mind that she felt were important. When she was close to completing the CD project, she contacted Amor Luz to ask her if she could schedule a one-on-one session with her during the Star Knowledge Conference for 2011 at Cahokia Mound near St. Louis. Amor had been instrumental in inspiring Emily to work on the CD, so she sent Amor a copy before the recording was even finished. Amor contacted Emily to say that she was amazed by the impact of the project and ask if she would work with her at the conference on presenting her workshops. Amor and Emily decided to confer in person before the conference took place, so Amor decided to spend a few days "on the way" from California to St. Louis at Emily's farm in Middle Tennessee. In preparing for the weekend in Cahokia, Emily felt something was about to happen, but she could not put her finger on it.

Amor came with her partner, Abel, and her two youngest children, who were in their early teens. They all felt it was important to have a ceremony. So, they built a fire and called in the directions to set a sacred space. Emily felt a welling up of emotion with an intensity she had never felt before. She knew they had to be released so she asked Amor if she wanted her children exposed to the powerful emotions that she felt coming up. She told Emily not to worry and that she would take care of them. So, Emily allowed it to come. And, boy, did it ever!

Emily said she would like to have been able to witness objectively what happened after that, but being the one experiencing it, she did not have that option. At one point, she dropped to the ground on all fours, and began to moan and wail and scream into the fire, breathing all the pent-up emotion into the flames. She felt the sadness and sorrow and pain of the ages of human existence move through her with a force that cannot even be touched with human words. Once it became evident that the moaning and sobbing weren't effective enough to process the enormity of what required processing, she began to speak light language. At this point, she was barely aware of what she was doing or what was going on around her. She was just letting it be, letting it happen, and being the vehicle and oracle for expression of the deep woundedness of humankind's collective experience.

This was way beyond her personal drama and pain; this was huge.

There came a point that she stood up and turned away from the fire and was overcome with a different light language. She began to speak it and it flowed out of her faster than her mouth could utter it. She felt her hands moving, and her fingers making symbols in the air (see the chapter on signing light language). She does not know how long all of this went on. It could have been seconds, or it could have been hours. She never thought to ask or look at the time. But, once it ended and she came back to being aware of her surroundings, she noticed that the kids were no longer with them. Abel was sitting in a meditative position on the opposite side of the coals where the fire had been. Emily was lying on the ground with her head in Amor's lap, completely spent of strength. Amor was performing some kind of energy work on Emily; she thinks it was Reiki.

Recently, she participated in a cross-continental conference call where Amor and some other people, who are able to read the Akashic Records, offered their gifts to answer questions for the participants. Amor spoke in a light language during her part of the call and someone else translated. The insights that she received from that interaction were invaluable to Emily and have helped her immensely to understand the multi-soul experience going on inside her physical body. Besides Amor, Emily had not heard anyone else speak light language.

During the Akashic records conference call, Emily received the message that she has two souls working together in this incarnation. The star being that is housed in her human being is not able to incarnate into a human body because it comes from a dimension that is beyond the scope of current physical dense matter. It has come to work at a planetary level. This was a rare occurrence in former days, and when it did happen, it usually took many lifetimes for the host soul and the star soul to integrate. With the help of ascension energy and light language, Emily and her star being soul are working toward accomplishing this task over the course of about ten years, in one lifetime. This explains the overwhelming intensity of the experience she had at the fire ceremony with Amor.

Birthing in the Spirit

When I asked Emily what purpose light language serves, she gave this inspired answer:

I have come to understand that light language is a language of the soul. It speaks to the aspect of our being that is already in a higher consciousness. It is not meant for the human mind to comprehend, as the human mind exists now at this time in this third-dimensional awareness. There are people who can loosely translate at this time because they are in a different place in the evolution of their soul's awareness. Because our higher consciousness understands the language, it can make use of the communications that are coming through to bridge between the previously untapped realms of divine knowledge and the third-dimensional plane to assist with the changes that are occurring as they happen as human beings evolve. These untapped realms have always been available, but it is only now that humanity is beginning to connect with them.

I also have come to believe that light language speaks directly to the cells and particles that make up density. My personal understanding about the shifts that are happening includes the idea that there are not only changes that cause our minds, hearts and souls to evolve, but that the actual physicality of our existence is also changing. This requires density to change its form and how it functions in time and space. I can barely grasp this concept, so I do not claim to understand all that is implied scientifically or how all of this will manifest.

Light language is not new. It is being re-NEWed in human awareness at this time in the evolution of consciousness, thus an emerging of many people calling forth the utterance of light language. Throughout the ages, many languages have held the codes of light language. The music of the Solfeggio and Fibbonaci scales are light language. In fact, all music before it was standardized to the 440 frequency was light language. The ancient "names of God" from Kabbalah are light language. The lost syntax of dead languages no longer used en masse is light language. Most of the native tongues from indigenous tribes all over the planet hold the codes of light language. The sounds of nature—the whistling of the wind, the roll of thunder, the call of the songbird, the howl of the coyote, the trickling of water, the crashing of ocean waves, the hoot of the owl, the crackling of fire, the mewing of new-born kittens, a deep breath exhaled, the humming of insects on a summer night—all of it, light language. It has been with us and carried us through since the literal dawn of time. This insurgence of light language coming through in spoken word with no apparent meaning is a reminder to listen with the ear of our soul. Light language is all around us all the time. Choose to hear it."

I want to put your mind at ease regarding the "strange" manifestations that Emily demonstrated at the fire. These kinds of "groaning and travailing" began happening for me and several others in an intercessory group of "prayer warriors" in 1995 or 1996 while speaking light language (we called it praying in the spirit). When it happened, we felt as if something was being birthed within us or on the planet. Light language is a tool that can be used to birth the New Heaven and New Earth.

Those who are familiar with the scriptures of the Christian Bible may be comforted by these words found in Romans 8:19-29.

For the creation waits in eager expectation for the children of God to be revealed. For the creation was subjected to frustration, not by its own choice, but by the will of the one who subjected it, in hope that the creation itself will be liberated from its bondage to decay and brought into the freedom and glory of the children of God.

We know that the whole creation has been groaning as in the pains of childbirth right up to the present time. Not only so, but we ourselves, who have the firstfruits of the Spirit, groan inwardly as we wait eagerly for our adoption to sonship, the redemption of our bodies. For in this hope we were saved. But hope that is seen is no hope at all. Who hopes for what they already have? But if we hope for what we do not yet have, we wait for it patiently.

In the same way, the Spirit helps us in our weakness. We do not know what we ought to pray for, but the Spirit himself intercedes for us through wordless groans. And he who searches our hearts knows the mind of the Spirit, because the Spirit intercedes for God's people in accordance with the will of God.

And we know that in all things God works for the good of those who love Him, who have been called according to His purpose. For those God foreknew He also predestined to be conformed to the image of His Son, that He might be the firstborn among many brothers and sisters.

Channeling Messages

In January of 2014, I felt impressed to speak light language as I went about my household chores. This dialect sounded different than my typical light language. The next thing I knew another dialect joined the conversation and two light beings were talking to one another through me, asking and answering questions. I was standing there as an observer, allowing my vocal chords to be used to express coded messages into the collective consciousness of humanity. There were two distinct dialects or strains of light language coming through, and I realized I was channeling. The voices were different from one another and the pitch and tempo of the language had qualities that set them apart from one another. (I am not an impersonator, and I was not making this happen. I was allowing, much the same way I allow my pen to move across the page when I am writing light language.) This conversation went on for about an hour as I walked around dusting, vacuuming, and doing laundry.

This experience created an upswing in my ability to receive messages from higher realms. I started receiving downloads almost constantly after that and they were coming in faster than I could write them down. I started carrying my voice recorder in my pocket.

Sending and Receiving Energy

We activate for ourselves the same energy we send out to others. If you think that what you are sending out through your thoughts or light languages is not having any effect, think again. A friend of mine energetically sent me a halo one day. I could feel the beautiful and intense sacred energy, but I didn't know it was a tangible object that others would be able to sense. About two weeks later, I was silently praying light language while sharing healing energy with a man I had just met. In his inner vision, he saw this circle of light and said, "Did you know you have a halo over your head?"

I woke up one morning while writing this book, feeling discordant in my energy field. I thought of those I had recently interacted with either via emails, phone calls, or dream time. Several people came to mind–one in particular stood out, and I knew I was feeling the energy of his struggles. Naturally, Miss Empath wanted him to be blessed and happy, but I was informed that he was integrating a new soul and needed to have his own experience with it. Like a butterfly struggling to emerge from a cocoon, everyone must travel their own path to oneness and do whatever they need to in order to free themselves from whatever is binding them. They have the ability to do this and we do not need or want to interfere with this process. If someone asks for help in treating a situation, go for it. Remember helping others is about *free* will, not *my* will.

I was instructed to send my friend a beam of light. Light is divine intelligence and it knows what to do in every situation. It will not violate free will; therefore, you can trust the language of light to support the highest and best outcome. I intended a beam of light coming from Source. I started seeing a metal searchlight canister beaming one stream of light toward him and another beam toward me. Then, I heard, "the light is inside you, not out there. Send it from your heart." When I did, I saw the light in me, and in him, grow and expand. I felt impressed to send him a shield of faith. When I did, a shield like a coat of arms appeared in his field as well as in mine. Then I heard, "Whatever you send out to others—even in light language—is what you also receive and activate in yourself. It is like a mirror reflecting your own thoughts, feelings, actions, and attitudes back to you."

My next instruction was to tap into the light language I had sent out to others and the energy infused into the writing of this book. I did so and immediately felt a rush of loving beautiful energy flow through me. I realized this is a tool to test light language and see if what we are sending out is pure.

I was in a meditation group where the leader introduced light language and shared a 20-minute audio of a woman speaking what sounded like rapidly repeated trance-like sequences of "B" sounds: ba-ba-ba-ba-be-be-be-be-ba-ba-ba-ba, etc. My husband found it quite annoying and thought it was inauthentic. I can't say that I enjoyed the audio or resonated strongly with it, but I thought perhaps there was an encoded message or that the Morse Code-like pulsing of the woman's voice carried a message for my soul. I didn't feel anything positive but I didn't feel anything harmful either, so I allowed myself to stay for the duration of the audio. I think one of the gifts that the hardships and shadow work of 2013 brought many of us was the ability to discern more clearly our own truth and distinguish the difference between the voice of our inner guidance and the voice of our ego. I have to admit that in this instance it was difficult to get my condemning monkey mind out of the way and truly discern rather than judge. You have to decide for yourself in each situation whether or not something that is being said resonates with you or is something you can accept as valid. You can typically trust that what you receive spontaneously and without anyone urging you is authentic. If you are sincerely seeking, authentic light language will come when the time is right.

What I have since learned is that letters, consonants, and vowels carry awareness like a fabric of sound and light that can be felt in the body. A client was depressed because he was having health issues. I listened to his speech and noticed all kinds of detrimental beliefs popping up. He was actually affirming that his body was old, wearing out, and that he expected to feel bad because of it. I did a galactic healing session on him, and after clearing some blockages from his mental field and body, I began to hear "v" words such as vigilant, valiant, vanquishing, victorious, vessel, vehicle, variety, variegated, virile, victorious, etc. As I said these words aloud, repeated syllables came forth: va, va, va, ve, ve, ve, vi, vi, vi, vo, vo, vo, vu, vu, vu, vie, vie, vie. I had him start repeating them as a mantra and I felt something shift. I encouraged him to pull the letters/sounds all the way into the cells of his body.

Synchronicities abound. Kelly Beavers shared her understanding of the letter E on the same day that I worked with this client. Kelly said, "If you lower your understanding of the letter E, this high energy will stabilize." I believe this principle is applicable to all letters and sounds. We can absorb the energy of the vibration into our body to make lasting changes.

When to Use Light Language

Have you ever had someone give you a gift and then tell you that you can only use it on certain days or when they call you on the phone? Probably not. Light language is a gift or tool that can be used in service to you, others, and the planet. It can be operated at your discretion. It's the same way for those who believe that the gift can only be used when moved upon by the Spirit. You *are* spirit!

> *And pray in the Spirit on all occasions with all kinds of prayers and requests. With this in mind, be alert and always keep on praying for all the Lord's people. (Ephesians 6:18)*

People have asked, "Should I wait until I feel the urge or should I attempt to make it happen?" My answer is "both." If you are honestly seeking to grow, learn, and benefit from the experience, there is no right or wrong way to activate or use light language. I use light language like a kitchen utensil. I stir the pot by speaking or singing anytime, day or night.

Comparatively, we can make a decision to pray, or we can wait to hear God say something. By initiating the flow, I speak to my guidance. By waiting for the urge, I allow my guidance to initiate the conversation with me.

Sometimes there is little feeling attached to my speaking light language because I am involved in another task. I may be in the kitchen chopping vegetables while singing in light language. This is what I call "praying without ceasing" and therefore I do not consider it disrespectful or rude. We talk on the phone while doing other tasks, right? Our conversation with Source is ongoing and every thought is a prayer that is moving toward manifestation.

> . . . *stir up the gift of God, which is in thee by the putting on of my hands. For God hath not given us the spirit of fear; but of power, and of love, and of a sound mind. (2 Timothy 1:6-7)*

At other times I find that place of serenity within my soul and speak light language from the depths of my being. These are the times when I stop everything and allow warm energy to flow over my body. Sometimes it is so intense that it brings tears of joy. Amenreu says when he speaks light language, it is like watching his physical body do something while he is observing. It's like a semi-out-of-body experience yet he is still present for the moment of spiritual connection. The physical body is the connection point. The mind is watching it, but is also participating in it. This describes the shift that I feel when I enter the higher dimensions behind the veil of this 3-D world. It feels trance-like, peaceful, and amazingly powerful. I am surrendered, but I am still in control of my body, mind, will, and emotions. I love to feel energy moving, many times before the sound even begins.

Star or light language carries codes for vibrational healing through DNA shifts and activation. Vast amounts of energy can move through to support healing modalities or to aid in prayer or meditation. It has been known to help align subtle bodies, shift energies in a space, raise vibration, expand consciousness, provide protection, help a plant or animal, or bring peace to a stressful situation. When I used it to treat a toddler with severe health challenges, I got a sense that I was clearing her parental DNA and removing entities and contamination from them and their electromagnetic field. Regardless of what changes we may see on the outside, there was a shift in the lineage and a clearing of imprints that created this child's suffering.

The energy that is transmitted through light language can be powerful, depending on who is speaking it, singing it, or writing it. I encourage you to use it as a tool for healing, blessing, communicating with Source, or to shift to a higher or more resonant vibration. Since it is not for show or entertainment, you do not have to be a good singer to use star language (although you may be surprised how beautiful your voice sounds.) It is the divine sound of creation coming through you, which is a gift from Source for the highest good for all. So, enjoy it!

In the next chapter, I will deviate slightly from our topic of light language to present my view of multidimensional aspects and how to begin to integrate them. I think this will shed light on why light language is being activated in so many people—especially in the last few months of 2013.

Chapter 5 ~ Integrating Soul Aspects

I'm hearing voices these days—lots of them!

My body was tired one day, and my guidance told me to lie in bed for at least fifteen minutes. I was busy and didn't want to stop what I was doing, but I knew it would be best to follow that guidance. I retreated. As I laid there, my ego, in cohorts with my taste buds, said, "Wouldn't you like to have a Dr. Pepper?"

"Too much sugar and caffeine," I said.

The ego team said, "A little bit won't hurt. You don't even have to drink the whole thing."

Consulting my higher guidance, I heard: "All things are permissible, but not all things are necessary."

A little while later I heard my guides say, "You can get up now. It's been twenty minutes."

By then, I was enjoying my respite. So, I replied, "All things are permissible, but not all things are necessary."

We all burst into laughter.

You and I are not crazy for hearing voices or having experiences that seem strange to those who choose to live in the old paradigm of separateness. The voices some of us have been hearing are the souls and aspects of our multidimensional selves in all lifetimes and octaves or realms of consciousness. We, as part of the hologram of creation, are coming "home" to our wholeness and we are having conversations with other souls and soul aspects.

In the simplest of explanations, the ascension is the rising of Earth into Heaven and the drawing down of Heaven to Earth. It means that the Earth and her inhabitants become one with each other and the cosmos. The body is the connection point between heaven and earth. That is why we are beginning to embody the multidimensional aspects of our soul from all lifetimes. There is really no separation in time; so, during this time of ascension they are being united and integrated into this present incarnation.

Integration, or oneness, does not mean every soul or aspect is exactly the same or that we must lose our personalities. In fact, quite the opposite is true—we are better able to offer our unique expression to humanity when we are in harmony with our multidimensional selves. As we integrate, we find that we have access to all the gifts and talents we have ever used in any lifetime. Since many of these souls and soul aspects are coming from galactic locations they have and speak their own language. Thus, many people are hearing voices and speaking new languages that they do not understand.

I received insight one morning while writing this book. It catapulted me into a new understanding of the body as a portal, not just a vehicle. There are many ways of explaining it, and this is just my interpretation. There seems to be a guardian personality (ego) that animates and sustains the body. Its job is to protect the body and exchange information with the non-embodied soul group, soul aspects, or mission team in the field surrounding the upper opening of the portal. I believe these are the angels, archangels, galactic light beings, enlightened ancestors, ascended masters, etc. that the Bible speaks of as a "great cloud of witnesses." They give instruction to the assigned soul (personality/ego), which in turn sends updates or reports back to the team about how things look from the human perspective. The problem is that this personality can be adversely affected by the events and programming of Earth life. The ego's aspects (inner child, critical parent, rebel, etc.) are archetypes of the human psyche. Naturally, these can create blockages in the communication between the embodied soul and its guidance team. As they are integrated, each aspect begins to perform its duty in a way that brings wholeness and cooperation between all aspects and guidance. For example, the critical parent becomes patient and loving toward the inner child, who is then allowed to express itself in a playful manner without being a brat.

> *Therefore let us also, seeing we are compassed about with so great a cloud of witnesses, lay aside every weight, and the sin (illusions and patterns of the old paradigm), which doth so easily beset us, and let us run with patience the race that is set before us. (Hebrews 12:1)*

There are "less advanced" beings, or what we might call dark or less-loving astral bodies/energies, archetypes, or souls/aspects. At the bottom of the portal there is an opening that was created at the "fall of man" when unkind galactic beings tampered with the human template and deactivated strands of our DNA.

I believe there are souls trapped in lower dimensions that desperately want to be free. The light in the more-evolved aspects of the soul are seeking to draw them out for healing and integration. We cannot cast them out or get rid of them—they are part of us, and they are making themselves known. Pretending that you don't hear their voices will not make them go away. Trying to banish or punish them or the ego does not work.

I found it helpful to interact with these aspects and the ego—to listen to what they have to say. You may be surprised to find that your "ego" or shadow side can help guide you to your truth by showing what is hidden in your subconscious mind. The critical parent within your psyche has a reason for being so over-protective. The annoying inner child, pulling at your shirt tail and trying to get your attention, can tell you what is coming up for integration.

As we ascend, we are actually drawing these aspects into the light where they are transmuted and their vibration is aligned with love. The ascension process can be messy as our shadow side emerges. This upheaval lessens as we surrender to the love of the Divine Mother (also known as Sophia, Goddess, or Holy Spirit) and Divine Father (Christos, God, Abba). This surrender allows us as divine children to balance our masculine and feminine energies in sacred marriage within our own hearts.

Astral aspects of soul contain greed, hatred, jealousy, rage, and other attributes that are "anti-Christ" or opposite of the light. They are arising into our consciousness, where we are hardly able to ignore them as they beg to be reconciled. The ascension is our transformation into "all light" and no darkness. When we are fully ascended, any access the dark forces have to the human psyche will be closed or sealed.

> *God/Goddess is light, and in Him/Her is no darkness at all. I John 1: 5*

The best way to deal with these aspects is to acknowledge their presence and invite them into the light. Instead of hating the darkness, have compassion and thank it for giving you the skills needed for survival in the old paradigm. Teri Jo Tinus says, "Whenever I encounter, Mara, or my demons, I make it a practice to invite them in for tea. 'Oh, hello greedy attachment. I notice how you come to visit every time I feel myself falling in love. Let's have a sit with each other and figure out how to find peace.'"

When our neural pathways are being cleared, certain aspects may seem to be in "take-over" mode. The voice of the past keeps repeating like a broken record or a song that is stuck in your head. Light language and the Reset Breath© can be helpful when you can't get an astral voice to stop. Our normal breathing pattern is an inhale followed by an exhale. The Reset Breath© begins with an exhale in order to signal the brain that something is about to change and we want it to pay attention. Breaking the cycle alerts the brain that a change is being requested and that it needs to integrate the new information that it is receiving.

Begin by counting aloud: one, two, three, four, five. Immediately exhale or blow out through your mouth. Next, inhale through your nose. It is important to bring your breath deep into your diaphragm, keeping your shoulders relaxed as you inhale. Next, exhale fully and completely through your mouth. As heart rhythms, breathing patterns, and brain waves are synchronized, the physiology begins to shift. You may feel this as peaceful energy flowing in your body.

There is a video of how to do the Reset Breath© on Brenda Williams' website, http://earthproject777.com, if you would like to see a demonstration.

Journaling or speaking with your inner voices can also be a healing process worth the work and time it takes. *Feelings Buried Alive Never Die* by Karol Truman is a good resource for giving voice to your "less dignified" emotions. *Writing Down Your Soul* by Janet Conner is another great book to help you hear what these aspects have to say. Wholeness occurs as you integrate whatever has been separated from the other aspects of who you are. Once all the wounded parts and shadow aspects are healed, transmuted, and integrated, the voices you hear will be in harmony with one another and you will be able to trust your internal guidance, which will be clearer and better than ever.

Non-Resistance

Life contains puppy kisses and baby laughter. It is our choice at any given moment to change our reality, shift our perspective, and create something new. Light language helps facilitate these changes. But sometimes, the lovely smell of roses is accompanied by the stench of rotten eggs. I heard my dad once say after someone "freshened" the bathroom with a room spray, "It smells like somebody crapped in a rose garden in here!" Such is life. Buddhist tradition integrates both positive and negative forces into unity and thus prevents a war between darkness and light, which is the battle that most religious traditions have capitalized on.

I've written about non-resistance in several other books, but I think I'm finally starting to embody it. I went on a hike one day with some girlfriends. We came upon a campsite, which turned out to be a sacrificial site, for we realized that the remains we saw in the ashes was the carcass of a dog. I was repulsed and saddened by the cruel act that had happened there. Later that night, I had recurring images of that scene and felt like crying. I knew I was picking up on that energy and I had to do something to clear it before I went to bed. I didn't feel led to smudge or apply my usual "energy-go-away" tactics. Instead, I allowed myself to connect with both sides of the incident. I not only sensed the sadness, fear, and victimhood of the dog, I also sensed the empowered energy of the sadistic perpetrator. I realized that I am just as capable of creating "evil" as I am of creating "good," and that one is not better than the other. Without labels and placing value on things, everything is what it is.

On the next page is a poem I wrote about the experience.

I AM that

I am the baby who cries and the mother who comforts
I am the abused child who becomes a bully
I am a black hole, imploding with life
I am the judge, and I am the one who is judged. I am the jury
who sent the innocent man to jail; I am the prisoner who
suffered in that cell. I am the one who set him free.
I AM that, and that, and that.

I am the rabbit chased, heart pounding, into his burrow; I am
the fox that lost his dinner
I am the fly trying to land in homemade soup, and I am the
swatter that smashes the fly on the table.
I am good-hearted humor, and I am merciless ridicule
I am empty, I am filled; I am the filling
I am good, and I am bad; I am all things in between
I AM that, and that, and that.

I am the crucified one; I am the one who drives nails
I am the sacrifice; I am the redemption
I am the way, the truth, and the life; I am the detour, the
falsehood, and the death
I am a loving god who bestows good gifts upon humanity; I
am the destroyer, who takes it all away
I AM that, and that, and that.

I am the one who practices dark arts; I am the one who sings
in the church choir.
I am despised and rejected; loved and accepted

I am the cow in a green pasture and the hand that feeds her
grain; I am the one who slaughters her and eats her for
dinner
I am river and stream, polluted and clean
I AM that, and that, and that.

I am the horse, and I am the rider; I am the path beaten by
hooves
I am the flower that grows between the cracks of concrete
I am powerful and weak, courageous and fearful
I am cancer that invades a healthy body; I am the miracle
that restores health
I AM that, and that, and that.

I am the wise one; and I am the stupid fool
I am male, and I am female
I am transgendered, gay, and lesbian
I am the heat of a scorching summer day, bearing down on
one who has no shelter; I am the one swinging in the
hammock by the beach. I am the hammock supporting the
one within me. I am the tree that the hammock is tied to—the
tie that binds.
I AM that, and that, and that.

I am love, kind and delightful; I am rage vengeful and spiteful
I am the one who sets captives free; and I am the one who
enslaves them
I am the frigid frostbite of the arctic snow
I am the flame that warms the Earth and heart; I am the fire
that destroys the dreamer and his dreams
I AM that, and that, and that.

I am light, and I am dark
I am the gentle breeze upon spring flowers that bob their heads in delight; I am the tornado that tears asunder, and has no regard for children
I am the whisper of a secret, the roaring of the angry sea
I am rain and drought, the stork and the grim reaper
I AM that, and that, and that.

I AM all of these, and I AM none of them.
I AM all that is and ever will be; I AM nothing
I AM Creator and creation
I AM one; I AM many.
I AM that, I AM.

And, as is expected, I got plenty of chances to put this non-resistant perspective into practice. I ordered Dragon dictation to make writing this book easier. I installed it on my computer, only to find that the program froze up when I finished the training session. I started over and repeated the training session with the same results three more times. I reinstalled the program and rebooted my computer and the entire thing froze and nothing about the program would function. I was aware of the frustration in my mind but they were not registering in my body. I kept thinking. "Wow! This is not upsetting me like it would have three months ago. So, I thought I had non-resistance cinched.

The next day, however, I was sitting in the drive-through at the bank trying to deposit a check. I have been with this branch for five or more years, but this time, the bank teller asked me for my driver's license. I struggled to grip the slick plastic card from between the tight window of my wallet, but could not pull the card out. I got so frustrated that I ripped my wallet while verbalizing a string of four-letter words. Then, I started laughing because I realized how ridiculous I was acting. I was able to quickly pull my vibration back into resonance with my higher aspect.

Every situation allows us to open our hearts and move into a new place. What if we began to see everything without judgment? We would realize that we are choosing our course at every moment.

Chapter 6 ~ How to Activate Your Light Language

Spoken verbally, light language can bring a message, blessing, clearing, or healing aligned with the highest good of a soul, person, animal, situation, etc. It can shift energy faster than any tool I've ever used! Sometimes, you may sense that a message is for an entire group of people; other times you may discern that the message is for the individual you are working with. Or, it may be just for you! Light language is two-way communication. You can speak to and hear from Source through light language. You can speak soul to soul with another person as well.

Light language can start spontaneously, as it did for one person I read about who was smoking some "herbs," or it can begin by intentional pursuit as it did for me. The ability to speak light language can begin during prayer or meditation, a healing session, a worship service, a sacred ceremony, chanting, or when receiving/giving energy work, massage, or other body work such as myofascial release therapy. It has even happened while having sex. By the way, using light language with your partner during lovemaking heightens spiritual connection and takes ecstasy to an entirely new level. One of the most common times for a person to open to light language is in a setting where it is being spoken by others. But, it can also happen when you least expect it. Starr told me she heard it the first time while shopping in Kohl's department store.

Spontaneous Ignition

Brenda Williams was driving down the road in November of 1995 when gibberish started coming out of her mouth. She did not know at the time what it was called, but she knew it had significance in the work that she was doing with off-planet beings. The language continued and she wrote down a few syllables. "Ja et ca ne la tu" means "welcome to the realm of the masters."

In the mid-1990s, Morningstar was a delegate at an international grassroots women's conference in Australia, where she had been saturated in the tones and colors of many dialects and the deep beauty of the theme "Women United for Hope, Healing, and Justice." On a few occasions after that experience, sometimes while driving, she felt the urge to open her mouth and express the heartfelt sounds in what seemed like another language. It felt good to let it come out. She didn't know what she had spoken, but it was intense and moved with strong energy through her body and spirit. As one who had battled a severe stuttering problem from the time she was a child, the new language came as a profound relief and a way of liberating and expressing her soul.

During the next decade she facilitated expressive arts groups where there were many opportunities to play with vocal improvisation, both sounding in words and singing, within a loving supportive container. Sometimes the sounds that came from within her and others during these sessions had a resonance that seemed to create an opening and a spirited shift for the whole group.

She went on a spiritual pilgrimage in January 2014 to Magnetic Springs in Eureka, Arkansas. In several days of "singing the waters" in healing rituals, much communion was shared as one by one the women were immersed, moved, activated, and healed by the sharing of these holy sounds. Light language came forth in Morningstar and some of the others who were in ceremony with her. Morningstar said, "Improvisation in all its forms—sound, poetic story, movement—have opened my heart and my consciousness to moment-to-moment contact with the movement of the holy. That's what I experience in my spirit most all the time, and I communicate and share it with others. Sometimes it's a light language. Sometimes it's just fully 'embodying the word' by opening the channel to the light—the essence of it. Then it can come through in spoken language, in dance, sound, and especially in the silence. It's all about energy."

Jennifer Hall was in a Reiki healing circle in 2012 when she began to feel energy welling up in her throat. Something was ready to be released and she wanted to allow it. The group facilitator had given permission for tears, laughter, groaning, or whatever was needed for healing to be expressed during their time together. So, Jennifer let the energy flow. Suddenly, she burst forth and began to utter new words, phrases, and syllables that sounded like a real language. She had no idea what was transpiring, but she felt a lot better afterward and knew that something had been released and was no longer holding her back. She played around with this newfound vocal expression over the next few days but decided that maybe it was best to just put it behind her, as it was a bit scary and not something she really understood.

Toward the end of 2013, she had another occurrence during a group breathing meditation. On that occasion she felt sudden strong energy from her solar plexus to her throat and spoke in the same language that she had in the Reiki healing circle a year prior. No one in the group seemed to mind and some even commented that it felt healing to hear her words. It happened a couple of more times during group meditation, but only when the breathing technique was involved. She talked with her friend Tina (a psychic medium) about it and they decided to do the same breathing meditation in hopes of it happening again with Tina witnessing it. Jennifer felt energy welling up in her solar plexus and throat so she began to speak light language to Tina. Tina said she could understand in her spirit what Jennifer had said and she also had a feeling of energy shooting through her. So far, Tina is the only one who has been able to interpret Jennifer's angelic language.

Jennifer's experience happened around the time that I posted an announcement about light language on my Facebook wall. Jennifer did not see that post, but our mutual friend, Joan Kuykendall, did. Two weeks later, Jennifer met with Joan and five members of the meditation group. During the breathing meditation, the language manifested through Jennifer again and she decided to allow the utterance. The group coordinator called it light language and said she had heard it before. Everybody in the group said they had gotten something from the language. Jennifer felt more comfortable speaking it. However, the dialect that came through that time did not sound so nice. Her voice sounded angry, almost chastising, so she wondered if this was of the light. Of course that disturbed her and she could sense that it might have bothered members of the group.

Jennifer did not desire to receive any negative attention but she wanted to continue to let the language flow. That negative-feeling incident prompted her to confide in Joan who was at the group meditation and had seen my post on Facebook. Joan directed Jennifer to contact me. I was able to help her understand what was happening and suggested it might be best to give an explanation of light language before allowing it to happen in a group setting. Even though it is accompanied by intense energy at times, we are always in control of how we use light language and when/where we allow it to manifest.

Some people repress light language and it goes away. However, it will come back if you open to it again. Repressing the urge might feel disappointing when you truly feel the need to express what Spirit is giving you to share. I remember sitting in church with a prophetic message welling up inside me so intensely that it felt like my diaphragm, chest, and throat were going to burst. Of course I had control of my body, mind, emotions, and behavior, but I felt that what I had to share was important. There was a good chance I would use "prayer language" (that's what I was calling it at the time) in the expression, and I knew that the church I was in would not appreciate the sudden disruption. There were rules in place for the expression of what we called the gift of tongues, and rule number one was that there had to be an interpreter present and one had to get prior permission to share a message during church services. Since I never knew when the urge would hit, it was hard to get prior permission. And, how would I know if an interpreter was present? What if the person who understood my galactic language did not attend the service that day? So, I went to the bathroom, locked the stall door, and let my message rip—very *quietly*. You don't have to be in the same room with the person(s) who are to receive the message. You don't have to be loud or boisterous about it. Because we are all connected in spirit, whoever needs the message and the activation it carries will get it energetically.

Jennifer and I met in November 2013 at Emily Singleton's ceremony for connecting with the 11:11 energy and time portal. Participants set an intention to personally align with the ascended Earth by opening a portal to Orion. I can't say if it was the opening of the Orion portal that created a greater cosmic awareness for me, but it was soon after this ceremony that I began to reactivate light language that I had practically ignored for years.

Who Can Speak Light Language?

> "I will pour out my Spirit on all people. Your sons and daughters will prophesy, your old men will dream dreams, your young men will see visions. Even on my servants, both men and women, I will pour out my Spirit in those days." (Joel 2:28-29)

Can anyone speak light language? Some say that only certain people can speak it and understand it. Personally, I think that anyone who has agreed to ascend has this ability within them. Everyone has light language because it is one way the soul communicates with its Creator. However, not everyone is *ready* to activate this universal language of light. Because it comes in so many varieties and flavors from singing beautiful melodic vowel sounds to making animal sounds, many people are using light language without realizing it. Anything that aligns with the vibration of light is light language. It is about *being* light in every word, thought, deed, and attitude we express. Light is the power of creation.

I like the way Emily Singleton put it: "Anyone, and everyone, has access to this higher form of communication without the need to look to anyone else. The words, 'many are called, but few are chosen' were actually meant to say, 'All are called, but few choose.' All that is necessary to receive direct communication from the Source and being-ness of ALL THAT IS is the sincere, authentic desire and request for it to happen."

When Will I Get My Light Language?

It's like being pregnant and knowing that your water could break any day. You really don't have control over the delivery date. I remember being nine-and-a-half months pregnant with my first child. I was ready to try anything to bring on safe labor. Walking did not help. Riding in a car on a bumpy road did not help. If I had not been induced I might still be pregnant! The same could be true with light language.

A person can be "induced" or activated by exposure to light language. One person activated when he heard the light language I spoke for him during a galactic reading (see weare1inspirit.com/light-language-readings). He spoke it non-stop for half an hour after the reading. Once you get activated, it will continue to increase. People often open to light language, or to new variations they haven't spoken before, simply by being around it.

Reactivation

Recently, I saw four women in one gathering open to light language simply by being around others who were speaking it. One had been hearing the words in her head and found the courage to speak them verbally. Another had been speaking privately. She let go of her reservations and spoke it within the safe setting of the group. Two other women had used the gift in decades past and didn't know they could still "do" it. I let them know that they could release the pause button and pick up where they left off. They both did just that before the weekend was over. How beautiful were the dialects each one spoke. It amplified the sweet energy we already felt in the group.

Despite the dramatic entrance of light language into Emily Singleton's life toward the end of 2011, there was a long period of silence that followed. Like many people, it was in the latter half of 2013 that light language reappeared in her life. She realized that this is the native language of the star being's soul that shares her body with the human soul born in it. She has two distinct souls that are individuated, yet not ate—they are so integrated they are actually one *being*.

94

Emily said, "I believe light language is the tool that is expediting the process for merging the star being and the human being within me." The use of light language privately has become a very normal part of her life. Recently, though, as her inner light begins to shine brighter, she does not feel as inclined to hide her light language under a bushel. She is cautiously stepping forward to speak it in public settings, either one-on-one, or in groups.

I was sitting in meditation one morning when I heard, "We are about to give you the Ascension Graces. I did not know what that meant, but I figured I might hear more than I could remember so I grabbed a pen and some paper. Then, I decided that hearing the words audibly would be the best way to share them. So, I opened the voice memos app on my iPhone and recorded what I heard. I later transcribed them phonetically the best I could.

If you would like to hear them spoken, please visit http://weare1inspirit.com/light-language/.

If you are unable to be around people who have light language in active use, the following ascension graces may activate light language in you. You may feel energy in your throat, heart, or solar plexus. Or, you may hear strange words in your mind. Let the energy flow and say the syllables or sounds aloud. Light language flows in and out of any sound, song, or tone you might feel moved to make. You may want to write down what you hear or speak and use this as a prompt if you need to get things going later. Occasionally, you may get a translation of the sounds, or you may get a gist of what they mean. Most of the time, there is no translation. That doesn't mean it is inauthentic.

Ascension Graces

Oh-ma ka ta-ta	Hear the voice of wisdom within
Ka-si-toh ma-ta-ta	Apply the wisdom of truth
She-la no-ma ta-tee-on	Answer the call
Jzohm ba-ta lay toin-da	Surrender and allow
She she ma cee ta	Expand your essence
Tha-ro-ma ta ish-on	Flow without resistance
Fee-la ma toh-da	Speak the codes you have been given
Toin da-la de-da moy-tie	Believe in your divinity

Shely Mort offers Source codes at expandingrealities.net/lightlanguage.htm that can help to activate light language by reading the words aloud. She recommends being open to it by talking "baby-babble" when you're alone. She says that the shower is a good place because the water enhances communication from behind the veil and with other aspects of your consciousness. Water conducts electricity, sound, and light. Shely reminds us that light language is not about learning anything or having a "correct" pronunciation of words. She encourages us to get comfortable and let the sounds of the language your soul wants to speak come through you into physicality as sound. "Spirit is about having fun and connectivity," says Shely, "it's never about rules or getting it 'right' or being 'holy.' It's about feeling 'wholly' present to yourself and feeling happy with your creative being. Play with it. Let go. Loosen up. Be spontaneous. Enjoy and experiment."[1]

Sound or vibration can bring forth healing. It can also activate light language. Connected to the ancient wisdom of native tradition and singing into the frame drum, Karen Renée Robb has awakened a spirit within that she did not know existed, and she is awakening that spirit in others. I saw this transpire in a frame drum class that she led. A couple of women started intoning vowels that morphed into syllables with consonants. When we were asked to make unique and non-melodic vocalization, Jess and I recognized light language coming through in other participants. I'm not sure these lightworkers realized what was happening or if they had already been using light language prior to the workshop. It was also interesting to hear animal sounds coming forth. They are quite fun! Who says only children can pretend to be animals? When we stop abiding by the rules that society expects adults to adhere to, we realize that light language is found in the tweeting of birds, the howling of wolves, the hissing of wild cats, the buzzing of bees, and all of nature as she sings her song of creation. I feel sweet energy all over when I hear Karen Renée sing. Hear or download Karen Renée's music at http://treespiritrecords.bandcamp.com/.

What to Expect When First Activated by Light Language

The physical and subtle bodies may have an emotional response to hearing or seeing light language. I have seen people burst into laughter, begin shaking, twitching, jerking, or having other bodily movements upon hearing light language. Quakers and Shakers, who travelled from Britain to North America, got their name from the "shaking" they did while speaking in tongues, prophesying, and manifesting other gifts of the Spirit, which awakened Kundalini energy. It is beautiful to see someone's countenance begin to beam, even through tears, at the hearing of light language. When this happens, it feels to me as if the Mother (Sophia) is bathing that soul with the light that emanates from Her heart of love.

The language of light is a direct means of communication between our higher selves and soul aspects, us and Creator/Creatrix, and between us and other people. It is not weighed down by ego, logical thinking, our individual stories, or personality. It is pure energy. Even before the sounds begin to come forth, you may feel energy in your throat or solar plexus. As you begin to release spoken syllables, your soul will likely feel the truth of the message even if your mind cannot intellectually understand it. Be with the heartfelt response; it may help you understand part of what is being exchanged.

Because it affects the DNA, the entire body is activated by the vibration of light language. The language of light activates the ability to remember our divinity and propels us toward our destiny. When I have spoken it face to face with another person, their facial expressions and body language seem to indicate an understanding what is being communicated at a soul level. Most people feel like they are "remembering" something they already know. It is not uncommon for tears to come as a response to hearing light language. Other responses to light language include, but are not limited to, shaking, jerking, groaning, crying, laughing, vibrating, tingling, rapid blinking, or a rush of sexual energy. These responses may indicate that your body is aligning to your higher self or oversoul as you access the upgrades now available in the template. These may be uncomfortable or frightening, but they happen because the body is not accustomed to having such intense vibrations surging through. Don't try to force things to happen; simply allow.

Not only is your body likely to have a reaction, so are your emotions and ego. These are only trying to protect you by telling you that star language is not real, not effective, or even something to be avoided. Remind these aspects that you, and they, are being treated with light and that there is no darkness in the light.

Speak Aloud

Brenda Williams says that writing or hearing the language in your head is not as effective in changing the molecular construction of the body, and therefore bringing in the highest aspect of the soul. While writing the codes is effective and can bring forth messages, it does not carry the vibration that is produced by the vocal chords.

> *"In the beginning was the word, and the word was with God/Source, and the word became flesh."* (John 1:1)

In the Christian Bible, God spoke things into form. Likewise, it is important that we vocalize light language and not just hear it in our heads or write the codes on paper. I encourage you to get comfortable speaking it, perhaps privately at first, and then in small groups that are ready to participate in this ascension exercise. This not only activates codes and changes our DNA, it creates a resonant field that can affect change in the collective consciousness of humanity. Light language is a bridge that connects us with our higher aspects, so use it to stay connected and keep your vibration high.

People may feel a strong desire to speak aloud, but often they don't because they feel silly or don't know what's going to come out of their mouths. It really doesn't matter what comes out. The light is divine intelligence and knows what it is doing. The more you practice speaking light language, the more comfortable you will get with it, and the more powerful you become in your ability to use it as a tool for healing yourself and others.

When new dialects or strains are activated you may sense that what is being spoken is coming from a higher being of light. Perhaps an aspect of your soul or someone in your soul group or guidance team. I found myself carrying on dialogue with two different dialects of light language. There was a call and response activity in which two beings were communicating with one another, asking questions and answering them. I speak in this language at home every day because I feel that I am speaking out what is being given to me from higher dimensions. These are activating me and others as they deposit information into the collective consciousness. These coded messages are adding data to a new program that is being created for mankind—one that will return the body to the Adam Kadman and return the mind, will, emotions, and spirit of humanity to its divine right order.

What Does Light Language Sound Like?

Galactic dialects, or "language of the angels" as Bryan de Flores calls them, sound different from speaker to speaker, and have recognizable patterns, syllables, and tones to them. Dr. Arthur Cushman, Medical Director at Quantum Neuroscience Center says, "There are several [light languages]: Arcturian, Pleiadean, Sirian, and the Light

Language spoken by the Elohim, Angels, and Extraterrestrials of higher Realms to communicate. This is the original language of man prior to the Tower of Babel. The Dolphins and Whales also speak Light Languages." [2]

Many times it begins with repetitive syllables, gibberish-sounding baby talk, or soothing songs. Try not to judge it as you allow it to flow.

The language of light has many different tempos, dialects, and variations of sound, pitch, and tone. Some of the light languages I have heard spoken are primal, low-pitched syllables that have a serious tone or even sound angry. At times, there is a sweet intensity that indicates the passion and significance of what is being spoken. Some are sing-song, Asian-like dialects; some use tongue clicks, have "tick-ety" or "chit-chit" characteristics; other have high-pitched fairy-like qualities. Many sound like the romantic languages of Europe, and others imitate bird, reptile, oceanic, or animal sounds. While it is not uncommon for people to only speak one strain, often when one dialect comes through, others will follow. The more you speak it, the more the language comes forth and the more powerful you become in your ability to use it as a tool for healing and spiritual growth. I have personally witnessed this as I give readings to clients who desire energy work and healing.

One of the most amazing things I have encountered with light language was when a woman and I sat in half-lotus with our knees touching. As we stared into one another's eyes, our souls connected through eons of time and dimensions. She did not blink for more than five minutes and her eyes never watered as she spoke a phrase and waited for me to respond.

She said the same phrase again and again until I understood that she wanted me to repeat her. It was not difficult because it sounded and felt like we were speaking the same language. When she started singing, I automatically started singing with her. The next thing I knew I was singing the exact syllables she was singing and matching pitch and moving note to note with her melody, which I had never heard with these human ears. This went on for more than a minute before I started sobbing, "I remember! I remember!" My soul recognized the language and song of my "home" in the stars.

You cannot *teach* anybody how to speak the language of light. However, I have repeatedly seen people initially activated or open to new dialects they haven't spoken before simply by being around others who are speaking it. If you are willing to allow your soul to intone the sounds it wants to speak, they will come through you. Remember, it is not necessary to understand what you are saying. Just let the flow of energy move to the right place in your body.

Many times we feel intimidated to hear ourselves speak or sing or to dance and move our bodies. We seem to have lost our voice through the childhood programming that creates poor self-esteem. When we can move past those barriers, we find that our light really starts shining upon the darkness in and around us. This gives us the opportunity to change.

Is Interpretation Needed?

Is an interpreter needed when light languages are spoken? When you are speaking it privately, there's no need for an interpreter. You will know what the sounds mean if you need to. There may be times when the interpretation is best to remain hidden, such as when the languages keep us from allowing our logical thoughts, limited perceptions, beliefs, and opinions from being misinterpreted. In a group setting, however, it may be beneficial to have a few people share what they sensed about the verbal expression. It can open a meaningful dialog when people are allowed to share how light language feels to their soul. We are sometimes limited by vocabulary when trying to express a message from another dimension. The languages make us *feel* and experience, instead of intellectually know.

Some people say light languages can't be understood at all or that the meaning is always hidden. While the energy delivers the information we need to connect with, there are plenty of times when I understand the gist of the message being spoken—especially when I speak or write light language privately. I rarely get a direct translation of the sounds when they are spoken by someone else, but I have seen others communicate with full understanding in a telepathic manner using light language.

> *So what shall I do? I will pray with my spirit, but I will also pray with my understanding; I will sing with my spirit, but I will also sing with my understanding. (I Corinthians 14:15)*

What syllables do you hear most in your light language? There may be repeated sounds, patterns, and syllables that you recognize as a theme. Brenda Williams says she can tell by the ending of sentences where the language might be originating from. "Tu" at the end of sentences may indicate Lemurian. "Ra" the sun god may be coming through in an Egyptian language. In speaking my light language, I have noticed "ka" and "nana" coming through quite frequently, which may be prayers for the restoration of the merkabah or light-body.

These languages could be the tongues spoken by Atlantean, Lemurian, other ancient Earth civilizations, or they could be galactic dialects. What they all have in common is that they move energy, bring healing, and unlock codes in the DNA. They are about positive change. Since there is only one "time," and that is the present or "now," all of these are really one language, which I believe connects humans directly with Source.

Use light language as a meditation tool to raise your vibration, to help you get through difficult situations, and to heal. Speak aloud until the words evolve into a dialect of light language and the speech becomes spontaneous. You will soon begin to notice how the energy feels different for each dialect. Practice in the car or try singing as you walk. This will help to stimulate the ability by activating the brain and toning the throat chakra.

This light language of mine, I'm gonna let it shine!
This light language of mine, I'm gonna let it shine!
This light language of mine, I'm gonna let it shine!
Let it shine! Let it shine! Let it shine!

Hide it under a bushel? No, I'm gonna let it shine!
Hide it under a bushel? No, I'm gonna let it shine!
Hide it under a bushel? No, I'm gonna let it shine!
Let it shine! Let it shine! Let it shine!

Chapter 7 ~ Animal Light Language

Have you ever seen two dogs mating? Ever noticed a cat licking its butt? If you abuse your dog, it will come right back and lick your hand. It does not have the inhibitions that humans have. Animals, especially in the wild, do not modify their behavior just because someone is watching them. This is known as the un-programmed reptilian brain, which is a good thing. Children also come in without the knowledge of what is socially accepted and what is not.

Humans were not intended to have inhibitions. The proverbial Adam and Eve were naked in the garden without shame. It was not until the "knowledge of good and evil" came into play that we started having shame, guilt, and fear. We have hang-ups because our thinking has been hijacked and the routing of our minds (not our brains) has caused us to perceive things from the outside in, rather than from the inside out.

The human brain, unless it is damaged, works the same way in every person. We have been programmed and have adapted to an agreed-upon system of accepted behaviors and we attempt to live within those parameters. Yet, not everyone acts the same way or believes the same thing, because how a person perceives is how that person behaves.

If we think light language is weird, or if we are afraid people will make fun of us, or not accept us if we speak it, then we will refrain from the very practice that could change the routing of our mind. We are unable to self-adjust our programming; we need help from higher realms. As we receive the upgrades that have been made to the human template, our routing will be restored, our DNA codes will be opened and activated, and our inhibitions and monkey mind will cease.

Even though they have been subjected to living with the consequences brought on by the distorted thinking of humans, animals still know how to self-adjust. They can tolerate weather extremes and survive where humans cannot. These creatures can help us ascend because their routing or thought system has not been tampered with like ours. Some of the crazy weather we have been having in the past few years has come to teach humans how to self-adjust.

Contrary to popular opinion, planet Earth is not in distress; it is self-adjusting and quite capable of taking care of itself. When a volcano erupts and burns everything in its path, it is not long before plants start to grow again. The elements—air, fire, water, soil—reclaim everything over time. However, all of creation is ready for humans to be free from the curse we have been living under.

> *For the anxious longing of the creation waits eagerly for the revealing of the sons of God. For the creation was subjected to futility, not willingly, but because of Him who subjected it, in hope that the*

creation itself also will be set free from its slavery to corruption into the freedom of the glory of the children of God . . . For we know that the whole creation groans and suffers the pains of childbirth together until now. (Romans 5:19-22)

Tree and mountain poses in yoga are about putting the body into a position that resembles some shape or movement of nature. While no yoga class I've ever been in has asked the yogis to meow or moo while in cat or cow pose, I don't think there's much difference between stretching like a cat and vocalizing like one. Many people believe that we have had incarnations on Earth as animals, fish, reptiles, etc. If that is true, then perhaps expressing animal sounds are a form of light language. Imitating animals can be an opportunity to connect with, or momentarily "become" the animal in order to integrate a lifetime we had as that animal. It could also assist animals in their ascension. It is not only the humans that are being transformed.

I remember hearing about a group of people at the Airport Vineyard Fellowship of Toronto barking like dogs, swooning to the floor, and laughing uncontrollably during services. The Association of Vineyard Fellowships, founded by John Wimber, expelled the Airport congregation from the Association for "going over the edge." This caused a split within the Vineyard Movement itself. I find it ironic that the Vineyard supports tongues, prophesy, and all the other gifts of the Spirit mentioned in the Christian Bible, but would consider people to be strange for connecting with the energy of an animal by imitating it. In my opinion, demons are counterfeit souls seeking to control by imposing their will upon another. When we try to control another person or reject them if they behave or believe differently, we are cooperating with dark forces. Remember the Crusades, Inquisitions, and witch burning days? All this was caused by people being deceived and controlled by dark forces. All our judgments toward self and others are a product of this kind of brainwashing. In writing this section about animal sounds I had to face my own shadow side and preconceived ideas about what is proper and improper behavior.

Tapping into our primal roots can return us to a state of innocence much like we were when we were children, before our parents, peers, religion, and society taught us how to act. All the fun is usually programmed out of us by the time we become adults. I realize that making animal sounds in church *may* be the result of someone desiring attention. Whether we are sincere or just showing off, making animal gestures and sounds, gives us a chance to work with a repressed aspect of our soul, bring it into resonance with the higher aspects, and work with the vibration of an Earth creature who is also on its path to ascension. This integration moves us toward the wholeness or oneness that we have spoken so much about.

While we would think nothing of children crawling around on the floor and acting like animals, it is unacceptable for adults in our society to do this, especially in a public setting. Unless, of course, you are in an Interplay group where adults are asked to let go of such inhibitions in order to find their voice and true self-expression. Interplay is a facilitated group that helps people get out of their heads and into their body through movement and vocal expression. To give you an example, I would like to ask you to do one thing. Get up from where you're sitting and get on the floor and start acting like an animal. Do whatever gesture that comes into your mind. Make whatever sound that wants to come out. As you make these animal movements, allow yourself to feel whatever you feel. Feel the embarrassment of being "caught" doing this; feel the playfulness and rightness of it. Feel it all and be honest with yourself as you ask, "Is there really anything wrong with this?"

This is not likely how you will show up for your next dinner party or for church on Sunday morning; however, let me warn you that something like this *may* manifest for you or someone else in a group where light languages are being spoken. So, please don't freak out or judge it immediately. Just sit with it. If you feel like joining in, then do so.

> *What you must do to move yourself into the mental framework for miracle working is to just let go. ~ Wayne Dyer*

During the dream weaver light language workshop in January, a woman tossed a rabbit coat to me and asked me to connect with the spirit of the animal. I did not know what animal I was holding, but I started growling and making a vibration with my tongue. Then the urge came to make a hissing sound. *Hmmm. I am definitely not holding a snake,* I thought to myself. I was in an environment where I would not be judged, so I allowed these and other sounds to come forth. Next, I got quiet and began to feel sad. I wanted to cry. I now realize that the hissing and growling sounds were connecting me to the energy of the predator. The sadness or sorrow that I felt was the grief that the rabbit's companions felt when they were taken from the herd. I also felt a trusting innocence that was probably from the rabbits who did not know they were about to be killed. (It takes thirty to forty rabbits to make one coat.)

This experience taught me a lot about how disconnected we are from nature, animals, and the Earth. Man has assumed a position of dominance over all other animals and can no longer feel remorse or have consciousness about taking the life of living creatures. Since that day I sat holding the rabbit coat, I have been able to connect with other animals, and more accurately feel the energy humans are putting out. But, instead of feeling this in an empathic manner that causes me to have pain in my body or have an emotional reaction, I am able to transmute for that person whatever is ready to be aligned with the light, then let go of the energy and move on. Empathic intuition is a very useful tool. When we are able to tap into the energy of another person we know when there is intent for deceit or lying.

As we ascend, we are reclaiming our ability to express ourselves from the very core of our divine being. We are becoming free of our inhibitions and returning the animal kingdom (including humans) to its original non-predatory condition as it was before the knowledge of good and evil entered the world. According to the Bible, in the New Earth the lion will lay down with the lamb and there will be no more death—not even for plants and animals. Get used to not eating food! Our fuel source for the light-body will be light—not sunlight, but vibration and sound.

Emily Singleton sees ascension as being a rising up of the physical aspects of existence into lighter realms *and* a "calling down" of higher aspects (including things like consciousness, spiritual understanding, and divine knowledge) into the denser realms. She believes light language is one of the tools available to connect these two actions and to merge with that which has not been able to merge prior to this time in the evolution of consciousness on Earth. This integration is the process by which a new reality of existence is created. In a nutshell, light language is a bridge between what is known and what is knowable. As above, so below. The body is the connection point between heaven and earth. It is the vehicle for ascension to take place in our species.

We, as a society, have lost the ability to connect with one another physically. Our hearts are breaking on the inside and we crave human touch, yet we are uncomfortable when someone gets too close. Our most personal contact in the workplace might be a handshake. We want to ask for a hug, but corporate policy calls it sexual harassment, so we refrain. This is one of the reasons I love cuddle parties so much (http://www.cuddleparty.com/). For about three hours, a group of preregistered participants have an opportunity to touch, caress, hug, and even kiss one another in a safe, non-sexual manner and feel an intimate connection with another human being. This can be very healing for the soul—especially for those who have been abused and are afraid of being touched.

Our judgments and suspicions have separated us from one another at a heart level. We fear rejection and trust no one. Truth is, the incarceration rate in the US is only 0.743 percent. That's not to say that there aren't dangerous people on the streets. But, overall, people are good-hearted and want the best for others. We have been programmed to keep our distance, not share our secrets, avoid certain lifestyles, believe certain doctrines, and do things to be accepted. As a result, we have lost our inner compass and we struggle to receive from our higher guidance.

I found this on Facebook and do not know who to credit for it. As an attempt to honor the one who came up with these beautiful thoughts and words, I will leave the link to the website, even though the music and yoga event has passed.

> *Prophets and visionaries are rarely celebrated or even welcomed as such within their environs. Family thinks you are the black sheep, neighbors think you are plain nuts and the community spins wonderful and reckless tales of your imagined notorious misadventures, brimming with danger and threat. But WE know who you REALLY are. WE SEE YOU. You are one of the Dreamweavers, threading Reality with intention, purpose and the possibility of the unprecedented. You are the PoetBard, telling the story of a new mythos and cosmology, one where every particle is sentient, aware and responsive to your call. You are the Vibrational Master, harmonizing, attuning and synchronizing as you work with energies unseen, frequencies still called into question by so many. You are the Heart-Centered Healer, bringing compassion, aid and kindly help; you bind up the broken-hearted and heal the lame and halt. You are the SingerSower, planting musical seeds into the spiral cochlea cornucopia of those ears that are open and responsive to your Song. You are a Passionate and Creative Lover, expanding the infinite possibilities for the expression of Agape, creating pleasure that melts minds and hearts and merges them all into a single hot amalgam. You are the Total Anarchist Rebel, refusing to live as subject*

to the tyranny of any law, prince, president or pontiff that offends your sense of the Good. You are the True Philosopher King, or Queen, the living embodiment of Sophia, the Wisdom Goddess, open to her influx and channeling her Wisdom into your world as your unique contribution of Love and Service. We Honor You, We Thank You, We Cherish You and We Welcome you into this Wisdom Tribe. Please sign up for our Evolvefest Community Newsletter at www.evolvefest.com

In connecting with the Earth and with one another, we recover aspects of our soul that have been lost or stolen from us. When we begin to undo and reprogram the hidden beliefs, thoughts, practices, and behaviors of the old self and old ways, undesirable things pass away and all things become new. The New Heaven and the New Earth are within us.

Maryanne Savino sums it up nicely with these words: "We're coming into alignment with the pulsations and rhythms of the New Earth frequencies. It is an awakening of soul expansion and soul ascension, assisting us to reclaim our magnificence and restore us to our natural state of harmony and balance with all of the cosmos."

Chapter 8 ~ Written Light Language

As a form of automatic writing or artistic expression, light language can also be written as symbols or created as art. "The symbols and script are the ancient forms for communicating volumes of information without having to read pages and pages," says Tracey Taylor, who first started to experience strange events as a young child when she had vivid "dreams" of being taken aboard spaceships. "These symbols are meant to communicate the nature of the macrocosm."

Lisa Renee says, "Within the trinity aspect of the Godhead, the Holy Mother's body contains the pure 'Cathar' which is the Creators' geometric symbol language that holds the Arc of the Covenant codes." I believe the Cathar is light language in all its forms—the surrendered heart, engaged in embodying the essence of all soul aspects, can access it.

The next time you are doodling, pay attention to what you are drawing. Are there symbols or pictures that seem to have a hidden meaning or carry an energetic message? You may or may not be able to interpret what you've written, but you may want to listen to your guidance to discern if there is a message for you. One day I felt led to draw light language in a circular fashion. In less than a minute a picture started forming and I was able to glean a message that had all kinds of significance to me. After that, I made writing in light language a part of my daily journal entries.

At the Walk-ins Among Us Nashville Conference in May 2013, I unexpectedly received a reading from a galactic ambassador (in-body starseed) who attended. She spoke in English, revealing accurate and confidential information, which confirmed several things I had been asking my guidance about. Then, she spoke to me in light language and wrote a message in galactic code. I could feel the energy in the code and the entire experience activated something for me. She interpreted her code to mean that I was about to move to the next level. I cringed because my experience suggested that moving to the next level required a clearing process that felt somewhat like a frat initiation. My spiritual journey did take a leap after that; and, true to course, it was fraught with many hardships.

As I started writing in code I noticed that some galactic symbols looked similar. I asked my guides if these symbols always mean the same thing when we see them repeated. They explained that just like the letter "a" in the word acorn does not sound the same as the letter "a" in the word astronaut, one small change in appearance (or tone, vowel, or consonant when speaking it) can alter the written symbol or code. In the English alphabet, a letter P becomes the letter R when a diagonal line is added. The appearance of letters P and B are different by one half-circle; but, the sound and the words they can form (and their meanings) are very different.

My guides went on to say that grammar and punctuation rules do not apply to light language because these are not words; they are creation energy. Other non-linear components such as the soul vibration of the speaker, their intent and purpose, how much energy is flowing during the process, moon phases, planetary alignment, etc. affect how something materializes in form—either written or verbalized. For example, you can use flour to make a cake. You can use flour to make biscuits. While these recipes both contain flour, they do not produce the same outcome. The result depends on how the "piece" is prepared, what other ingredients are added, and who is making it. An unattended third grader making cookies at home without a recipe is going to get a different product than a gourmet chef in a commercial kitchen. When compared to the art produced by the masters, there's a vast difference in the art that most of us create.

What Does Written Light Language Look Like?

When I tried my own hand at writing code, I instinctively started at the right side of the page and moved to the left. Precise and separated symbols appeared.

When I started writing this book, I came across more written code and it activated me. I felt more connected with my writing after that. It still was not flowing—it still felt contrived—but I kept going. Soon, I had a set of symbols that I was *trying* to make appear in random repeats. My guides told me to "practice these and we will give you more." *Okay, so I must be on to something,* I thought. I continued to write and the next thing I knew my pen was starting to move as if it had a mind of its own. I had never done automatic writing before but I suppose that is what you would call this type of writing.

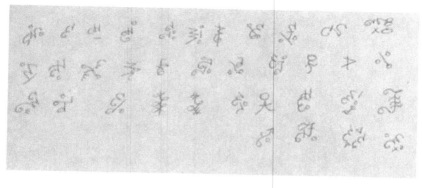

Yvonne's Early Attempt at Writing Light Language

After that, I started using fewer words in my journal entries, which had formerly been several pages each day. Instead, I would put a subject at the top along with the date and then speak light language while writing codes and allowing my pen to flow of its own accord. An amazing thing happened as I prayed for different people; the codes started taking on new forms and I was getting English words to go with the symbols. Sometimes my dialect would change and different-looking symbols would start dancing out of my pen and onto the page. I could sense a shift and know that whatever topic or person I was treating had received what was needed and the process was complete. I continue to be amazed at how I feel the energy moving through this fun and simple practice.

The English words that were coming through felt relevant to the person I was praying for. So I started doing galactic readings with light language and written code. When my friends reported how helpful the readings were to them, I started offering the readings on my website. These include one written page of code with some English words that remind the recipient to seek further interpretation. An accompanying MP3 file allows a recipient to hear the light language I speak as the code is being scribed onto paper.

Multidimensional beings and galactic messages do not typically come to us in sentence form. They use vibration, symbols, ideas, images, and concepts that are communicated telepathically.

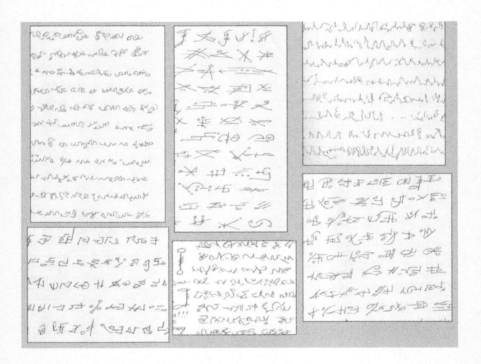

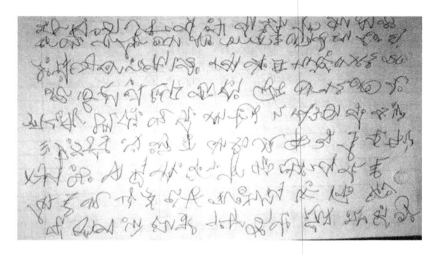

Yvonne's Automatic Writing

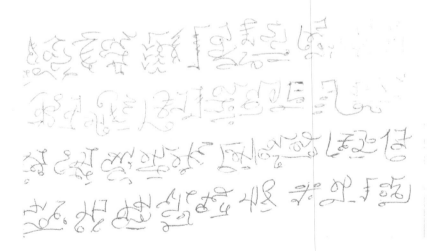

Written Light Language Samples

Written light language can take many forms. The symbols may repeat randomly or they may be unique and seem to have no uniform pattern. There does tend to be an overall style that each person develops.

When I saw a sample of Amenreu's written light language in his journal, I felt an energy surge and wanted to touch the page. It felt like I could connect kinesthetically with a message from the cosmos. Amenreu wrote galactic code on the rafters of the porch he helped us build.

I have included two of my favorite writings from Amenreu's journal.

Amenreu's Writing

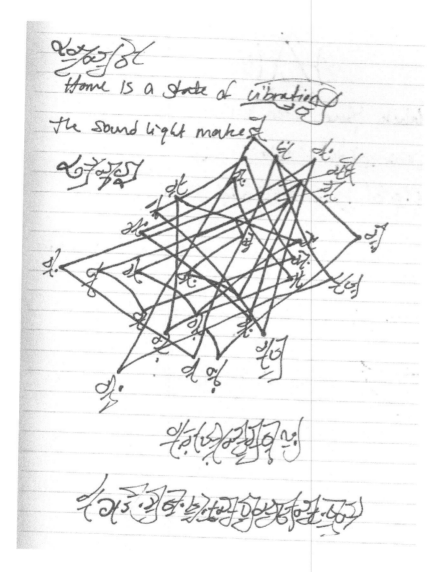

Home is a state of vibration

The sound light makes

Amenreu's Code Writing & Diagram

I was away from home on the cloudy day the roofers were laying the decking. Our neighbor across the street took photos of the work in progress and texted them to me. In one photo there is a "shield" of light over our house. I was encouraged to see physical evidence that my meditations are creating something tangible. I regularly visualize our home and all who enter being protected by light.

Mazuin Mynrose specializes in healing with a thorough cleansing from A-Z. She was born with the natural ability to perform healing by accessing the spiritual energetic plane. She started as a clairvoyant tarot reader, and soon recognized her potential as a medium and healer, able to send messages of love and peace from loved ones who have crossed over. On the next page is Mazuin's written light language. See Andromeda Love Story on Youtube or http://tinyurl.com/Mazuin.

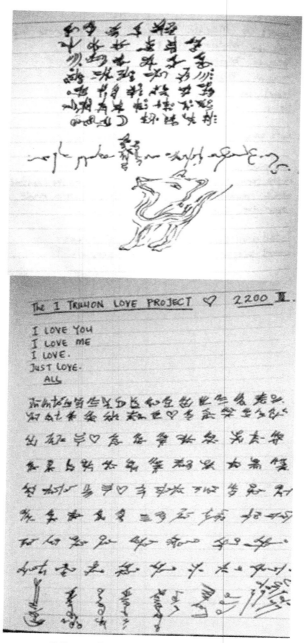

Mazuin Mynrose's Writing

Maryanne Savino is a ritual temple dancer and chantress, womb priestess, sonic alchemist, and intuitive empathic channel. She and I are such a vibrational match to one another. When we spoke on the phone it seemed we had known one another all our lives.

You might enjoy reading "The Ascension Process ~ Spiritual Evolutionary Journey into Higher Consciousness" on her website, www.sacreddanceandsound.com.

Connect with Maryanne on Facebook:
https://www.facebook.com/maryanne.savino

Maryanne Savino's Light Language Art
Codes of Light and Galactic Heart

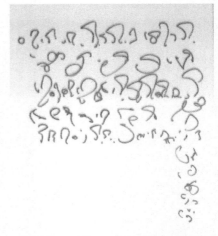

Betsy Nelson likes beads and prayers. Fortunately, those two things are more related than she ever realized. In her blog posts, she may explain something using beads rather than words. "I string together words the same way I string together beads, and both serve the same purpose," says Betsy. She works at a library and tutors ESL kindergartners. Betsy's understanding of God is derived primarily from Christianity, Judaism, and Buddhism, but she also reads Taoist and Hindu texts and finds a soul-friend in Rumi, the 13th century Sufi mystic. She

likes to draw, paint, collage, and study world religions. When she saw my post on Facebook about light language, she showed me one of her light language paintings. She also speaks light language.

Betsy Nelson's Light Language Art

Find Betsy online at http://betsybeadhead.com or visit her Etsy shop: http://www.etsy.com/shop/beadedretort.

The art that Vara Humphreys (http://varahumphreys.wordpress.com) contributed here is what she used in Chapter 7, "The Key to the Etheric" and Chapter 8, "The Key to the Wisdom of the Ethers" of her book, *The Science of Knowledge* (Ozark Mountain Publisher). As with all of what she manifests in sacred geometry, nothing is measured. She draws with a ruler and something circular.

Vara writes her script from right to left and looks similar to one of my styles. When I first saw her sample, my solar plexus lunged with excitement, like my team had just hit a home run. Her code felt familiar and activated something within me.

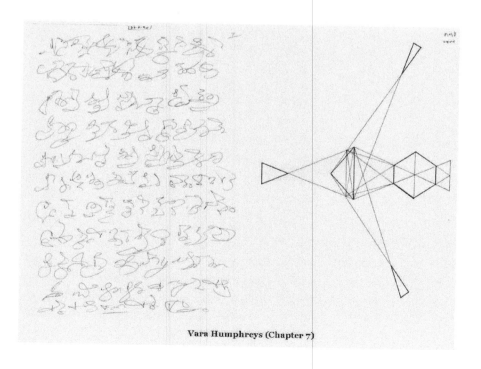

Vara Humphreys (Chapter 7)

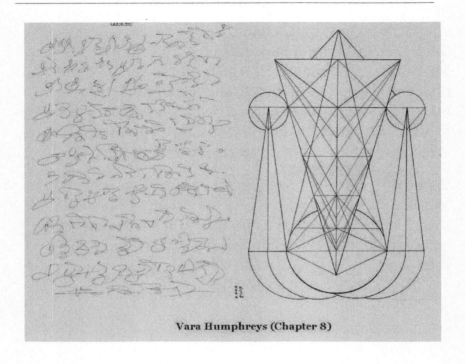

Vara Humphreys (Chapter 8)

Dr. Salo Stanley is a chiropractor, sound therapist, musician, artist, and intuitive from Fresno, California. After a spiritual awakening (walk-in experience) on a crystal healing table in Fresno, CA in 1992, many spiritual gifts emerged, including the ability to make contact with other beings in the Universe. She understands the nature of symbols and what she calls galactic light language symbols from our galactic communities. She is also able to see, draw and interpret these symbols, which come from our galactic communities out there in the universe.

Orbs are sometimes loved ones and sometimes ETs showing themselves to us in a non-threatening way to help us expand our level of acceptance and grow in a multidimensional way. There is a video Salo did with one piece of her artwork explaining the energy for 2014. She asked light beings to assist with the artwork. At 2:14 into the video, a light orb appears out of the center of the mandala http://www.youtube.com/watch?v=45gHcyWvXSA.

The following galactic light language art was created by Dr. Salo Stanley, D.C. It was drawn with color gel pens on black paper.

Salo's symbols create a visual stimulation for the right side of the brain to download these images. The right side of our brain is our feelings and intuition and bypasses logic. A silent telepathic sound is created when viewing these symbols. The basis of a symbol is trying to teach you to absorb a charge of light to our DNA. When we attract light, our dreams come true.

These pictures transmit a frequency in your energetic field. They download little files of multidimensional teachings and increase our human consciousness to connect with our higher self. They create data from the Galactic Library and other far-away planets in the Universe to help humans evolve. The frequencies of these symbols also connect us more to our guides, angels or teams in the Universe. It helps us become more self-empowered, upgrades our DNA, and dissolves old patterns and thought forms that no longer serve us. Visually looking at them helps to increase our frequency and light. It creates a major opening activation and energy portal within our energetic fields.

Many of these drawings are like fractals, caught in an expanding moment of time expanding. When people purchase these prints or drawings, Salo holds them between her hands to ask with heartfelt intention that the light beings come and live in the artwork to aid and assist the highest potential for the person it is going to. I love that!

See her art prints at http://www.salosounds.com/light-language-buy.html Salo's Etsy store is http://tinyurl.com/SaloEtsy. Facebook https://www.facebook.com/salo.stanley.

Seeing Salo's art prompted me to pull out my portfolio from an elective course that when I was earning my Bachelor's Degree in Metaphysics from American Institute of Holistic Theology in 2003. Here is one sample of light language mandala art that I created.

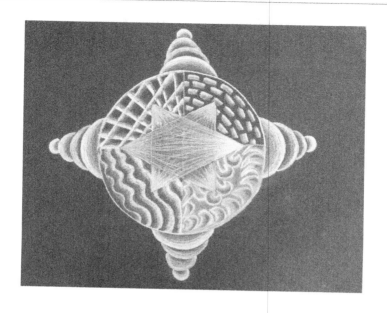

Clown, artist, singer, and songwriter Astelle Anomellarun was born in New York City and now lives in Ireland. She had a soul exchange process that was completed in May 2013. She created this beautiful light language art on her frame drum.

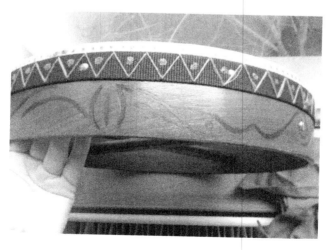

Pure joy and expansion are the feelings Karilyn Gomez (karilyn.gomez@yahoo.com) experiences with light language. Speaking or scripting symbols, she feels the rich depth of the multidimensional information flowing, as well as the lighthearted nature of the communication! This weaves through all that she is, whether it is expressed as astrology, tarot, and energy work with her treasured stones and crystals or enjoying the connection with the elementals in nature walking her dogs.

Karilyn is a Level 3 Certified Practitioner with Suzy Miller's Awesomism Certification Process, which focuses on connecting multi-dimensionally with the collective consciousness of the children (on the 'awesomism' spectrum), building resonance and coherence. As you can see from her light language sample, lightness is Karilyn's keynote.

The light language above was written with sidewalk chalk by a five-year-old boy named Abner Bray.

Try your own light language art or symbols on this and the next page.

Chapter 9 ~ Light Language through Movement

"If we hadn't a voice or a tongue, and wanted to express things to one another, wouldn't we try to make signs by moving our hands, head, and the rest of our body, just as dumb people do at present?" ~ Socrates, in Plato's Cratylus (Fifth century BC)

Have you found yourself playing with your fingers in your lap during a meeting or phone call? If you pay attention, you will notice that almost everybody does some sort of signing, but most people keep the motions small. What if you were to allow yourself to move your body as spirit directs? That is known as light language through movement.

Sign Language

It is believed that Native American communities, prior to the arrival of Christopher Columbus, used one or more signed systems to communicate with neighboring tribes. According to Wikipedia, the first recorded history of sign language as a visual method of communication in Western societies was in the 17th century. However, no particular person is credited with having "discovered" or inventing sign language. So, where do you think sign language came from? The same place light language comes from—the Creator.

There is an artistic form of expressing light language through the use of hand gestures, hand mudras, facial expressions, miming, dancing, and other body movements that look similar to the way one uses sign language to communicate with a non-hearing person. Like written and spoken light language, "signed" light language or heart gesturing as I've heard it called, does not have a consistently interpretable meaning that can be replicated by learning certain movements. All the movements are spirit led. Yoga and Tai Chi stir up and move energy by positioning the body to align with the energy already in the body as well as to collect more energy from Source and bring it into the body. This can also be considered light language, as it works with energy.

Unlike learned sign language that has a standardized system that can be replicated to consistently mean the same thing, the ability to sign in light language does not employ letters of the alphabet (fingerspelling) or use recognizable signs to represent ideas or words. It is a language of the soul that uses movement to communicate soul to soul. Many times, the meaning or the message will be interpreted differently by each person.

Jamye Price shares beautiful signed and spoken light language messages on YouTube: http://tinyurl.com/JamyeSigning. I have shared these videos with people who report being very moved by them, as was I. There is something very powerful about combining hand movements with spoken light language. When I first saw Jamye signing in a video, I jumped up like I had suddenly remembered I had something in the oven that needed to come out! With no effort at all, I started making the signs as if I had been doing them all my life. My soul strongly felt and received the messages and I now use signs frequently when speaking light language. I could not resist the urge to contact Jamye at www.JamyePrice.com. I was overjoyed (literally) when she responded so graciously. I asked her how she got started signing light language. I will share her response with you:

> *Light language first began signing through my hands as I was doing energy healing on clients in 2003. As the client lay on the table with their eyes closed, I would watch as my hands began to move on their own; swirling and 'writing' over the body, though I didn't recognize words. I had never been exposed to light language, so I had no idea what was happening. It was fascinating and surreal to feel my body moving spontaneously. I was already clairaudient, so I asked my guides what was happening. I received no answer, except to tell me that only about 40 people on Earth were doing similar work. Over the course of a year, my guides would answer only with a number of people doing similar work, and it would go up and down. Opening to light language was to be a journey of trust and choice for me. As the fluctuating number indicated, it was a choice to continue. At first it was intriguing for me since I was the only one aware of it, but soon the sound began pressing to come through. I just didn't know if I had the courage to be that odd. But life had other plans.*

One evening at a channeling event I had arranged, I burst out of the Light Language closet I was hiding in! By this point I had discovered what it was, but I was still reticent to allow people to see and hear me doing it. There I was in front of a group and it exploded through with so much force and volume that a teenager in the room started crying and one person had a spontaneous Kundalini experience that caused fits of laughter. I was mortified. Everyone was kind and supportive, but I just didn't know if I could go through that again. A few days later I did a session for someone from the event and I found myself suppressing it like before. My guides said to me, "It's alright, you can hold it in. It will just take him longer to heal." If I continued to hold it in, the restrictive energy of embarrassment and fear would inhibit my ability to flow energy to my fullest. That was the turning point for me. I came to realize that I get to live a normal life—I can go to the grocery store without erupting into light language—yet I have access to a special communication that goes beyond words. I spent many years discovering the nuances of light language and I grew to love it more than I could have imagined. Over time I recognized that I could speak many variations, write it, and even translate it, when applicable.

It took me many years to grow my courage to fully come out of the closet with it, though I did try to sneak back in there a few times! Each level of sharing light language seemed monumental to me. From clients, to classes, to audio recordings, to Youtube—I had to find new reserves of daring to expose myself as such an oddity. Yet the profound energy flowing through and the loving, tangible response from others always made me glad I didn't choose to turn back. It has changed and improved my life and the lives of so many others in significant ways. It's more than just a healing technique. It is an indicator of a new level that humanity is reaching, as our capability to communicate with each other and our surroundings reaches new heights.

I have no qualms about sharing light language now, as I realize I'm offering a direct communication from Source energy that comes in many varieties. Most say that they recognize it even though they can't understand it. Many are brought to tears of love and remembrance. I channel galactic, angelic, and elemental energies as appropriate, allowing the wisdom of universal flow to create through me. I see people healing and opening exponentially, and light language is a vital part of the gift of our awakening. Now, rather than embarrassed and afraid, I feel honored to be part of this evolution of communication. It continues to evolve and expand, just as we do. The language is love, the vehicle is light, and humanity is becoming both.

Dancing in the Light

Maryanne Savino says, "In ancient times, temple priests and priestesses navigated into other worlds. They entered altered states of consciousness through sacred dance and sacred light language sound to align with the universal forces of creation. Mother Earth was greatly honored and loved, and the priests and priestesses knew that through embodiment of the sacred feminine and awakened masculine, one could attain harmony and balance with all life."

When I am speaking light language in my prayer times, there needs to be some space available because my body is going to want to move. Pacing back and forth, walking in circles, dancing, or making gestures that hint at interpretation have been common for me since the mid-1990s.

Dancing is another way to create light language through movement. In my church days, I participated in an intercessory group that used light language on a regular basis. We were not well thought of because of our unusual mannerisms that occurred when Spirit moved through us. Many of us felt pregnant with creation energy and "birthed" in the Spirit. Several of us moved our bodies prophetically in a way that seemed to have a story or message being shared. I witnessed this again in Sedona when a Cherokee/Lakota grandmother named Sakina Blue Star, danced in our private medicine wheel ceremony. Seeing this activated something in me and I went into a birthing session that allowed many of my Cherokee ancestors who died on the Trail of Tears to go into the light.

"In dancing light language, we are reawakening memories from the ancient past, when temple priestesses danced for healing, pleasure, and transformation," said Maryanne Savino. "I feel that it's a divine remembrance from deep within the cells to awaken our unique gifts as we dance the path of alchemy. As we speak and or sing these codes of light, we are birthing a new beginning and recreating ourselves.

"Light language inspires movement and empowers us to live in alignment with our divine purpose. Rather than giving a performance, I see it as 'PrayerFormance,' a prayer in motion to embrace and embody our divinity. It can be used as

Divine Mother transmissions, which are circular, serpentine, and infinite movements that emulate feminine power. Some of the dances are expressed in an organic spontaneous way, while others are guided movement sequences that connect us with the multiverse."

Because light language is only decipherable within the sacred heart and soul of every human, it cannot be taught. Therefore, I did not plan to offer any "how-to" instructions in this book, but when Spirit is in charge, we learn to change our plans and keep flowing. So, this next section is here to give suggestions as to how you might activate light language through movement and bring more effectiveness to your meditation or healing practice. It came as a download during an energy treatment that I offered a friend through a text message.

We started with some deep breaths to get the body into a space of receiving. I felt into his energy field and found some heavy, sad energy around his heart. I don't automatically move stuff like that unless I have permission to do so; therefore, I asked if he was ready to release it. He agreed, so I started speaking light language to his heart. Of course, he could not hear this because we were texting.

I heard "Lon-*nay*-ah, light as air." At first I thought the mantra was just for him. But, afterward I realized that it could be used by anyone who wants to treat themselves (or others) with light language in a very gentle manner. I instructed him to repeat the phrase again and again. His field and chakras opened up and the heavy energy he had been carrying released and was transmuted. The energy continued to expand and he texted to say he felt trance-like. So did I.

After a few minutes of basking in this light, I was asked to have him stretch, dance, move into yoga asanas, tai chi, or do any kind of movement that felt good while continuing to repeat the mantra. I reminded him that if other sounds or syllables wanted to be expressed to just flow with it.

It occurred to me that this spirit-and-body movement was bringing the mantra or light language into the cells of his body. Light wanted to speak to the cells and bring them into alignment with the pure vibration he had tapped into.

Many times when we meditate, we go into the ethers and experience a beautiful expanded state, but then we leave the energy there when we return to our daily activities. This is why the "high" one gets during a session may not last or make permanent changes. It is important to bring that higher state of awareness into the body so it can vibrate within the cells in order for code activation to occur. The more we are in our body, the more we can embody divine master presence. The goal of ascension is to bring Heaven down to Earth and Earth up to Heaven—not to fly away! The body is the connector point between the two.

There was another level that needed to be integrated in this session with my friend. I had him get still again and feel the expanded energy around him and in his field. Then, I had him draw that energy through his body and into the Earth as an offering of love. Next, I was instructed to have him pull Earth energy into his body, making his body a connector point between the Earth and the higher realms, thus creating a very nice balance. He stayed with this process until it felt complete; then he went about his day feeling refreshed and alive.

An acorn must send its roots deep into the earth before it can grow upward and hold the weight of becoming a stately oak tree. The same is true for us as we ascend. This is why we are integrating all aspects and doing our shadow work in preparation. We have to go down and connect with the Earth and integrate the body and personality with the higher aspects before we can go up and hold the vibration of the higher dimensions.

As above, so below. Stay in your body and connect deeply with the Earth. Go outside every day and put your bare palms or feet on the ground and tell Mother Earth that you love her and appreciate her life-sustaining energy. Personally, I do not think it is helpful to send into the Earth (or anywhere else for that matter) any detrimental energy that is being released. No one wants crappy energy coming to them! If it's not serving *your* highest and best, it is not serving anyone else's either. Instead, ask that detrimental energy be transmuted or converted into beneficial energy that can assist with enlightenment and connect us with the Earth in a loving and healthy way.

As Lisa Renee stated in "The Song of Christos Sophia" in February 2014, "To arrange, activate, and transmit the [Mother/Sophia] Arc codes, individually and on the planet, requires the sacred heart tone of Mother's aspect activated fully into the Sophianic body of the earth." As children of Sophia [Mother Earth] and Christos [Cosmic Father], we are the vessel that contains the presence of both masculine and feminine energies.

I encourage you to use this practice and this mantra, or another one along this line, to create a full-body meditation

143

experience anytime you choose. It activates DNA codes and allows you to access the upgrades that have been made in the template of the human form and then bring those peaceful vibrations into the Earth as you connect with her water, air, fire, and soil. You embody more aspects of your higher self each time you send love to the Earth.

Don't be surprised if more syllables/mantras come through in the following days after practicing this, or if you have the urge to make some strange kind of vocalization. Get your mind out of the way and let the vibrations of your higher self flow through. These are continued activations that allow more of your higher aspects to be housed in your body.

So, get up and dance, move your body, and try new positions as you speak light language.

Chapter 10 ~ Children Who Speak Light Language

Did you pretend you could speak in foreign languages as a child? My friends and I spoke Pig Latin (Ig-pay Atin-lay) when I was in middle school. It was fun to create new words and communicate in a unique way by taking the first of a word and moving it to the end followed by the "a" sound. Star children, indigos, crystal kids; some of them speak light language at an early age. Mary Rodwell says that these cosmic humans are highly intelligent, perceive other realities, see unusual beings or strange orbs of light. They have a sense of mission and demonstrate healing abilities; they also write unusual symbols, and speak in strange languages that feel more comfortable than the language they have learned to speak.

When my step-granddaughter was a baby her babble sounded like Chinese. No matter how many times we corrected her, she continued to call me Ho-Ho. It occurred to me that she might have known me by that name in a past life. However, I did not like being called a "ho" or be thought of as the belly laugh of Santa Clause. This frustration continued for months until she finally learned my name. While writing this book, I made an art piece with light language symbols and hung it in my office. My husband was looking at the piece one day and pointed out a "HoHo" symbol. Perhaps the baby babble that we think is nothing more than an infant practicing their vocal abilities and trying to learn to talk could actually be their native galactic language or a language they knew in a past life.

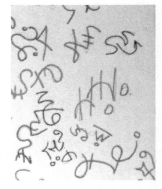

In a dream, I saw a fly with a man's face. The fly didn't know he had wings and could become airborne, so he just sat there. Because he had assumed a man's face, he thought he had also assumed man's limitations. Isn't that just like us behind this veil of illusion? We wear an Earth suit and therefore we think our soul has limitations. When we realize we are divine, we know we can fly beyond our perceived limitations. Children do not know the same limitations that we have adopted through subconscious beliefs and social teachings. How do we keep our children pure and less affected by the world system? We teach them a new norm.

Angi Gaian Progeny was about four years old when she started speaking light language with her imaginary friend. She was bored a lot as an only child, so she tapped into a male presence that she felt was always near her. She couldn't see him, but she could feel his presence distinctly. She didn't want anyone to know what she and her imaginary friend were talking about, so she made up a language that sounded like babble. When she tried to teach it to the neighborhood kids, they called her weird, so she stopped doing it until she got older and had more self-confidence. Angi says her tongue sounds like a mix of Native American Indian, and Asian dialects (mostly Japanese), all mixed in one. But it has traces of other idioms as well. Music playing in the background will significantly alter the dialect.

When her son was an infant (he is now four years old), she would sing lullabies and speak to him in light language, and he seemed to understand her. She also talked to him telepathically. As he got older, he became more fluent in speaking light language than in speaking English. If the child was doing something wrong, Angi might more easily say, "Ah nau ko pauna she hass anoh!" than, "don't touch that; it's hot!"

Her older kids would look at her a little funny and say, "You're crazy, Mom!" She told them it is the language of the angels, fairies, mermaids, unicorns, etc. "Angels speak in your head," she told them, "and if you were to hear them out loud, this is how it would sound: 'neeeeeeeeeeeee' (high-pitched sound). And, faeries sound like this: 'fau sha li na.' They were much more interested in it then. They don't generally speak it spontaneously, but Angi hears them all do it from time to time. She would like to record some music in this language someday when she has more confidence for public exposure.

As a child, Alison Hodgson was constantly bullied at school. One day she felt emotional energy welling up inside. She opened her mouth and words flowed forth without her mental input. She was shocked by what had taken place and does not remember what she said, but the words were kind, mature, and direct. The episode stayed with her ever since due to the impact it had—the bullies never bothered her again. She was abused as a child and found comfort in speaking her own language. She would fall asleep talking to herself like this when she was young. She stopped doing it around her friends because it sounded silly to them.

She would speak the light language at home until her mother told her, "Those words aren't real. Stop making them up!" She did not stop using her language—she just did not do it around her mother. Although she received no verbal response from her guides when she spoke it, she always sensed their responses and associated peace with it.

Alison knows there is energy and power behind those undecipherable words and says the language is an important part of her life. Like receiving a message during meditation, the words come automatically and without involving the thought process. Speaking light language is how she got her star name, Kristarlis.

The first time she felt the urge to speak it to her husband she was concerned about how he would react. She took a leap of faith and let the words flow. She was surprised when he replied with the same language. They laughed about it, but it was such a light and happy feeling that they continue to do it every night before bed.

When Jess Bray first spoke light language to her son, he spoke it back to her as if it were the most natural thing in the world. And, why is it not natural for the soul to have its own language? I believe it is time for this form of communication to be fully activated to enhance the next phase of human evolution. It enables us to communicate more fully with the crystal children now coming onto the planet.

Chapter 11 ~ Accessing Upgrades

Recent upgrades in the template for the human body are coming online through a second group of starseeds who were born into the body or walked in during childhood, teen years, or early adulthood. Some names for them include indigos, crystal children, rainbow children, and star children. These hybrid (human and starseed) beings remember being on spacecraft, talk about "home" as somewhere besides Earth, and display unusual healing gifts and supernatural abilities. They are literally changing the vibration of human consciousness just by being on the planet.

The concept of time, future and past, is going away as we heal and integrate all aspects of our personality into a unified whole and begin to live in the present moment. Even if you are not a starseed or a walk-in, you are likely being affected by the shift in consciousness we are experiencing on earth. Things are changing rapidly, but there is still a need to move gently. Should everything in our DNA shift all at once, we would likely start seeing, hearing, smelling, tasting, and sensing in other dimensions. We would create all kinds of personal chaos and global catastrophes if all of our thoughts manifested instantly. And, just think what would happen if all of our lifetimes were consciously experienced simultaneously. Talk about schizophrenia! We would no longer be able to function in the world. Let's be thankful the DNA reprogramming *doesn't* all happen at once. The ascension is a process of remembering; it is not a destination.

> *"The ascension journey was created to help us remember who we are in our truest nature . . . Divine beings who chose to have an Earthly life at this time . . . to really experience this unique and amazing process . . . light languages have helped me to remember my starry origin. Being in a human form gives me the opportunity to experience deep sensations in body while remembering that I am a star/light being"* ~ Maryanne Savino

While the upgrades are present in the template for the human body and are accessible to us, it will require some intentional integration and collaborative engagement in order to bring them fully online. At this time, there is little of that going on, but we are making progress. Something shifted energetically on January 1, 2014 and many empaths felt it. As a result, we are better able to maintain calm within the chaos whenever we encounter the personal field of someone who is out of peace. This is especially helpful to empaths who tend to pick up energy from other people. We are realizing more and more that staying in peace is not about putting up shields; it is about choosing not to engage with external chaos and to diligently maintain peace in our personal fields. We know when we have to disconnect from someone and avoid having contact with them as they are having their experience with integrating their shadow side or lesser-evolved soul aspects. These are all steps that move us from confusion and disharmony to emotional stability and peaceful resonance. Already, some of us know how horrible it feels to be out of resonance with our higher selves. The "signals" are instantly recognized and we are able and willing to make an adjustment and realign quickly. We realize that our emotional state is a choice. With the misaligned period shortened, the physical body is able to function at peak efficiency and with little or no interference or stress on its systems. And, that is physically evident. A friend of mine posted a photo of herself on Facebook. People were astonished and commented on how youthful, peaceful, and joyful she looked.

No timeline has been established for the changes in mass consciousness to happen. It is an inside job. Some will evolve faster than others and will reach back down the ascension ladder to help those who follow. There is no need to worry about others. We will all eventually ascend and understand the universal language of light. Most of us are still at the previous integration period. Many lightworkers are bringing in the upgrades ahead of the curve, but things may not look much different outwardly (politically, economically, socially) for a while. Few people in the general population are able to assimilate the changes many of us are experiencing inwardly. That's okay. We are not here to change the world; we are here to *be* the change we want to see in the world.

The old paradigm is defined by guilt, separation, judgment, clinging, competition, us and them, right and wrong, God and us, human and spirit. The new paradigm is defined by connection, truth, love, playfulness, oneness, inner guidance, rebirth, peace, compassion, freedom, allowing, forgiveness, acceptance, confidence, community, receptivity, letting go, living fully present, and being comfortable with not knowing. Like Amenreu said in his foreword to this book, "The ability to behold peace is that of an individual's experience, but the ability to manifest peace is the decision of the masses. The masses may be influenced, but swayed only by their desire to be aware of peace and for their neighbor to also be aware of peace." When we have intimacy and integrity with ourselves, everyone else will know it. It will ripple outward from individuals and create overlapping circles until the entire body of humanity is awakened.

Having said that, it is true that unless we engage one another, these insights and postulates will not come forward in the masses. We need to hold peace in our personal fields and share peaceful resonance in group settings. Brenda Williams is doing this in the phone calls she has been conducting to hold resonate fields across the world. EarthProject777 is about our personal, global, and universal evolutionary process and how to move collectively into a more resonant and collaborative field. Brenda has brought forward a process that supports a merging of our higher awareness and our physical form without the inner conflict that has been present within the body in the past. You may contact Brenda at http://earthproject777.com for more information about participation on the phone calls.

This collaborative work is also being done in sacred circles like the ones I've participated in. You may want to get involved in a local group that is doing healing work. Check Facebook, Twitter, Meetup.com or other online groups to find out where in-person meetings are taking place. Ask Spirit to guide you to your tribe.

Or, you could start your own group. From 1995 to 1997, I was part of a prayer group in Indiana that created a resonant field and saw many miracles manifested as a result of our prayers made in one accord. We can create whatever we like as long as our personal field is in alignment with the universal field. After I left Muncie, I felt a loss for the ministry team and their uplifting and loving energy. In January of this year, I felt led to start a group where people can share the visions and dreams they have been given individually and see how their pieces of the puzzle fit together. We plan to use light language to help bring our dreams into form as we support one another in the bigger picture.

I encourage you to start or get involved in a circle or group in your area and begin to hold resonate fields that will help to bring the template upgrades fully online. Practice speaking light language together as well! You may be surprised how fun and effective it is.

Chapter 12 ~ Letting Go of the Old Paradigm

We don't need to remove the old paradigm in order to live in the new one. The New Earth may not look much different than this one. It is not a change in external reality. It is a life lived from the inside out—a shift in awareness in the relationship we have with ourselves. From outer focus to inner knowing. Not living from the head but living from the heart. This allows us to know our oneness and the truth of who we are. Naturally, this will change the way things look on the outside and in our world. The only shift that needs to happen is within us.

The body was not created to process intense emotions. As you ascend you may notice that you have emotions in mid-range where the highs are not as high and lows not as low. This smaller variation of highs and lows is what antidepressants seek to accomplish. Even in this state of less intense emotions, we are aware of our feelings and acknowledge them. We allow them to coexist in harmony. We may feel anger and still be smiling; we may feel joy and not have any facial expression that indicates the bliss we are feeling inside. In other words, we are becoming masters of our own feelings and emotions. Before this process is in place, however, we may experience some tremendous highs and lows to help us notice what is coming up to be integrated.

Once the emotions stabilize, we no longer feel the need to rescue others or take on their emotions to help them process them.

I had a dream that I was in high-rise apartment with my grandsons. One was twelve years old and the other was four years old. We were eating white bread and junk food, and I was sorting through some laundry that was not mine. The next thing I knew I was in the driver's seat of an old car, but I was not able to steer the wheel. Someone else was controlling the vehicle, so I asked them to drive us back to the apartment because I had left the food and laundry there. My grandsons and I got out of the car and went inside where we found other people tending to the things I had sorted. That's when I looked around and saw that my four-year-old grandson was missing. Panicking, my older grandson and I started looking everywhere for the little one. Was he still in the car? Was he in the parking lot? Did someone grab him when I wasn't paying attention? Did he get off the elevator on the wrong floor? I awoke from the dream and heard my guidance say, "Let go of the past. Stop sorting out stuff that does not belong to you and ingesting things that do not nourish your soul. Allow other people to deal with their own stuff. Pay attention to the things that have value now."

I have spoken with empaths several times about whether or not we should instantly jump in to heal or help another person. I felt that we should always ask before we take action. My truth about that changed when I read Luke 4:25-27 from the Christian Bible:

> *I assure you that there were many widows in Israel in Elijah's time, when the sky was shut for three and a half years and there was a severe famine throughout the land. Yet Elijah was not sent to any of them, but to a widow in Zarephath in the region of Sidon. And there were many in Israel with leprosy in the time of Elisha the prophet, yet not one of them was cleansed—only Naaman the Syrian.*

This scripture seems to suggest that we should be selective about who we offer healing or help to, but upon further inquiry my guidance showed me how this is actually referring to being led by the spirit and knowing when and where to show up. It is about how to listen well in order to be in the right place at the right time to help others.

You may remember the sorrowful hymn, "O, Sacred Head Now Wounded." I can relate to wounded heads. One day in meditation, I started hearing the lyrics in my mind. "What language shall I borrow to thank thee, dearest friend?" Light language? Of course! Then, I heard the following message, which I believe applies to all healers, not just me:

> *O, sacred head, once wounded and now healed, you have been anointed to proclaim good news, set captives free, recover the of sight of those who are blind, relieve the oppressed, and to proclaim the year of God's favor." (Luke 4:19) "Be the light. Maintain the vibrational frequency in your personal eighteen inches and keep your lamp trimmed and burning bright.*
>
> *If you turn on the overhead light in a room, the table-top directly under the light will get more light than the area underneath the chair in the corner. But, the entire room is affected to some degree. The light in you will shine upon all darkness and whatever is ready to receive light and shift, will shift. Unless you feel certain that you are not to get involved in healing someone, know that the answer is always yes!*
>
> *Raise your own vibration, for if you be lifted up, you will draw others to the light and they will be set free without much effort on your part. In any*

situation you find yourself in, you can trust that "wounded" heads (mental thoughts) and souls have been drawn to you for healing and help.

May you have eyes to see what Spirit is doing. May you have ears to hear what Spirit is saying. Be the light. Proceed with joy in all things.

That was pretty clear guidance but my past experience with helping others as an intercessor was reminding me of the "backlash" of negative energy I took on as an untrained empath. Even though that has not been occurring for me in quite some time, I realized I still had fear around doing energy work on others. Yet, I was feeling a call to begin my work as an energy healer. I saw a post on Facebook in which someone was requesting healing vibes and prayers. My guidance wanted me to take action. My fear wanted me to not get involved. I steered clear and went to bed, but I didn't sleep well that night because I kept thinking about it.

The next morning, I was reminded of the request for healing. I spoke with my guidance and acknowledged my fear of repercussion. That's when I heard this message:

Your body is the temple of the Holy Spirit, not a target for an enemy. There is no enemy, unless you create one. You say you are protected, and you are, but we ask you to consider what it is that you feel you need to be protected from. You are light and in you dwells no darkness. This is truth. Your fear is not. If you focus on being attacked, then you can create that experience for yourself. If you focus on being empowered you can experience that. It is your choice. Whatever you send out is what you receive in return. When one person heals, you and others are also healed. For "the many" is one.

I was speechless for a moment while that sunk in. Then, I made a choice to be the light, heal those who cross my path, and listen well to know *how* to proceed. So, I felt the fear, spoke gratitude for its voice, which brought this misalignment to my attention, and then I sent healing energy to my Facebook friend. And, I started offering energy work to clients.

Once you own something as your personal truth, you gain a new tool to work with. What is your guidance asking you to let go of in order to gain something even better?

Chapter 13 ~ Weaving Soul Aspects

As souls, we are divine expressions of the Creator's consciousness. Therefore, we are multidimensional aspects of one Source. Some of our soul aspects are living in a body (not always a human form) and other aspects are in spirit in other dimensions and realities. At this time of ascension we are able to access more frequencies and octaves or realms of consciousness. As a result, we are able to sense the presence of many soul aspects and communicate with them as we collaborate on a common mission of restoring oneness.

A purer (more evolved) aspect of our soul can join a body and walk along with the incarnated soul. Sometimes the purer aspect will reside in the electromagnetic field of the body and assist as a guide. There may be times when it seems an aspect or guide temporarily swap places as his or her energy, wisdom, and talent comes through. In these cases, the residing soul does not leave, like what I believe occurs with a soul exchange. When there is deliberate cooperation and clear communication between the soul aspects, one member may access the "driver's seat" of the consciousness as needed to accomplish certain tasks. You will notice subtle shifts in energy, personality, skill sets, etc. as the soul with a particular talent best suited for the job takes the wheel or instructs you as they watch over your shoulder. Some stay "at the wheel" for a few months or years; some only a few hours or days. Many people are unaware of what is occurring, but they feel this shift and are somewhat concerned about what they are experiencing. Characteristic vibrations or energy signatures of these other aspects come in with these shifts and it can be unsettling for someone who is uninformed about this "weaving" of soul aspects.

I have discovered that I can ask for an aspect to assist me with any situation. When that aspect comes in, I feel an energy shift and start to express myself a bit differently. When I'm channeling information from higher realms, my personality and frequency is different than when I'm playing with my grandchildren. My body also feels different, my breathing pattern changes, and an alternate dialect of light language may come through.

There are times when the soul born into the body may need to take on another phase of the mission. To do so, it leaves the body in the hands of another member of the soul family, either temporarily (known as a placeholder soul) or permanently. If the cord of light that tethers a soul to the body is disconnected and a new soul's cord of light is connected, this is known as a soul exchange or walk-in. This can happen suddenly or over the course of a transition period. The soul now in my body (76-99) reappeared in August 2011 but did not take the wheel back from the placeholder soul until 2014. Many times the physical body and emotional body will grieve for the soul that left. Soul exchanges can create some radical changes in personality, likes/dislikes, relationships, jobs/career beliefs, etc.

For example, since November, 76-99 has started speaking in three strains or dialects of light language as was her custom while she was in the body from 1994 to 1999. I felt a loss of time and it still seemed like I was in the decade I had been in previously. I had lunch with my ex-husband for the first time in fourteen years. When I come across things that 76-99 owned, I would hear her say things like this: "Oh, she kept that!" or, "I remember that bowl from the Oak Road house," or, "Where is my piano?" (That piano has been at my daughter's house for five years.) One morning, 76-99 inquired about a jacket she wore in the 1980s. When hanging on the doors of the refrigerator and looking for something to eat one day, I heard, "She stopped eating meat?!" I feel like an observer as she unfolds and acclimates, yet she *is* me and I have complete jurisdiction over my life.

Soul exchanges are more dramatic than soul aspect weavings. Many people are beginning to experience aspect weaving and the many accompanying voices, skills, character traits, and gifts. Soul exchanges do not happen to everyone, but we are seeing this occur more and more these days—many occur during sleep and the person wakes up feeling strangely different and may have opposite likes and dislikes than the former gatekeeper. For more information about walk-ins and soul exchanges, see walkinsamongus.org.

> *Signs of the times are everywhere, and there's a brand new feeling in the air*
> *Keep your eyes upon the eastern sky. Lift up your head, redemption draweth nigh!* ~ Gordon Jensen

I realize that not everyone reading this book has had a soul exchange—in fact, most have *not* had that experience. And, not all my readers are starseeds either. However, many are integrating future selves and multidimensional aspects of the soul, which can have a similar effect on the body, but to a lesser degree. I refer to the starseeds, who walked into adult bodies between 1970 and the first few years of this century, as "forerunners." These souls worked with galactic technicians who monitored the body's response and made adjustments as a higher soul aspect, future self, or another member of the soul group took up residence in the body as the born-in soul was ready to leave. These were pre-incarnation agreements to serve humanity in this manner.

Those who walked in back then may have felt confused and disoriented. We had little support to help us understand what had happened to us. We knew something was different, but because we inherited the conditioning, programming, cellular memory, and personality of the former soul, most of us did not have conscious knowledge that there had been a transfer of soul consciousness. Some had misalignments in the connection of the cord of light that sustains the soul's connectivity with the body. That made it difficult to stay in the body—especially when the body was suffering with biological malfunctions that were set up as an "exit point" for the born-in soul that was ready to give up the body for this galactic science project. The Earth's grid adjustment was not complete then, and interference in communication prevented accurate transmission between the off-planet technicians and the embodied starseeds.

Even those who were consciously aware that they had walked in were many times unable to let the galactic technicians know what was happening; therefore, fixing anything that went wrong was not easy. Then, psychic gifts started opening up and the confusion worsened as these starseeds in human bodies started seeing, hearing, and feeling disembodied earthbound souls. Those empathic and compassionate beings who gained the ability to tap into another person's thoughts or emotions were overwhelmed to say the least. Our bodies took a further hit when our ability to heal or transmute dark energy allowed energy vampires to tap in and drain us. If it reads as though we went through hell, believe me, that *is* how it felt many times, and there were very few people we could talk to who would not think we were crazy. Fortunately, there was Walk-in Evolution (WE International), a support group for walk-ins, started by Liz Nelson in 1994. I became the president of that organization in 2012.

The first batch of starseed walk-ins did some remarkable trailblazing in spite of hardships. This paved a way, making it easier for those who now are accessing template upgrades and integrating soul aspects with the body and personality. The bodies of some of the "veteran" walk-ins are now conditioned to hold purer vibrations, either more evolved soul aspects or starseed souls.

From what many of us sensed, a group of starseeds from Andromeda arrived on the planet sometime around New Year's Day. A group from Pleiades arrived at the end of January, and more from Orion were to arrive in late February. No wonder galactic languages of light have been activated! This influx will likely continue as more resources are called to help us merge Earth and Heaven.

You may be feeling the reverberations from this influx of starseeds. This has activated light language in a good number of people. Some of these starseeds are beings from 12th dimension and higher but they are unfamiliar with 3-D Earth life and how things function here. They come in with a lot of knowledge but we are asking them to use wisdom in not pushing forward too fast with their mission. In order to avoid repercussions later, the body and personality need time to be integrated with this higher vibration these souls are bringing in. It would be helpful to hold resonance and peace in your personal fields. Suggestions for holding resonance include the following:

- Get into or near water. Take warm showers, use hot tubs and steam rooms, swimming pools (depending upon weather—indoors), and sit/walk/stand by lakes, streams, etc. Drink a lot of water.
- Stand near fireplaces, burn candles, have bonfires, etc. to connect with fire energy
- Deep breathing to take in fresh air to all the cells of the body. Get outside and breathe as much as you can, even it if is only for a minute with a heavy coat on. We know it is cold in the Americas.
- Get into nature every day, put your bare hands or feet on the ground—concrete will do since it is made of materials from the earth. Sand trays, stones, crystals, plants etc. in the house.
- Animals that are raised in torturous conditions and are violently slaughtered carry a vibration that is wildly chaotic! Putting that vibration into a body that is already adjusting to rapid change is counterproductive to holding a resonant field. It is true that plants have just as much consciousness as animals, but plants (other than GMOs) are more likely to be attended to by hands that love the earth and support her as she supports us. Use your discretion and see if this resonates with you.
- Use light language: speak it, write it, dance it, sing it, draw it—bring in the codes. Move the body gently— yoga, tai chi, stretching, dancing, and other forms of

gentle movement. Aerobic exercise is not necessary (or harmful).

- Speak kindly and lovingly to your inner child (it may seem like the ego is acting out). These aspects are afraid of what is happening or they are ready to heal from past experiences. Speak to these aspects and help them know they are loved. Lift them into the light with the gentleness of a mother tending to a baby or child.
- Meditate and listen carefully to your inner guidance before making any changes to the daily constitution of the life you inherited. Some are in religions, relationships, locations, etc. and will help these situations shift by staying there. If the body is in danger, of course you will want to make changes, but we are asking everyone to listen, listen, listen and let your off-planet support know what you need!

Your mission will unfold naturally, and your path will be much smoother if you lovingly tend to the personality and care for the body. Otherwise, your vibration may be so intense that people are actually afraid of you. Love is the answer to that dilemma—love for yourself, the Earth, and others. We are bringing purer frequencies of our future selves and their aspects to live in our human form. At the same time, we are bringing the body into perfect health as its structure is adjusted to maintain crystaline form in purer dimensions. As above, so below.

The following poem, copyrighted March 3, 2003, is used by permission of its author, Veronica O'Grady.

In the Lineage of Kings and Queens

In the lineage of kings and queens, more ancient than the sun, were born leaders of races and of the worlds to come. Long before Vikings and Camelot, and the Druid priestess fair, ancient hearts beat in rhythm with fire, water, earth, and air.

The memory of the stars beat strong in their breasts. Gentle eyes, strong love, and passionate, true hearts. Queens and kings in unity, harmony, balance and peace, creating worlds with agility, wisdom and ease.

Then a shadow cast its way across the earth and veiled the memory of our sacred birth. A forgetting slumber dimmed our sight, thus began the journeys, through the dark and the light. Forgetting and remembering cyclically unfolded, until these days of the awakening dawn.

Ancient ones awaken, my friends! Time to remember who you are! Rise up! Rise up! A new world emerges and with it our soul's dream. Here upon the earth, at this moment in time, the old cycle of fear is now complete.

Illusion is gone, clarity's light is bright. Truth becomes clearer. New breath carries the memory of the ancient dream awakened. And the reason we chose to be here.

We wake. We walk; remembering now. Breathe deep the gathering dawn. We are those ancient queens and kings from long ago. We are them, here now, reborn.

Here to fulfill our destiny. Here to fulfill the sacred dream. Here to create heart to heart, a new world. Here to create love's peace.

So as we tune in to the new cycle upon this earth. Light and memory again, emerge. The shadow's grip is now broken upon this graceful planet. Ancient ones, it's the time of our rebirth!

The technology of love is energy vast and deep, feeling dreams alive, with breath focused is its magic secret. Hearts strong, we create with love's passionate purity. Hearts united, we create this new world's new loving unity.

In the lineage of kings and queens, more ancient than the sun, were born leaders of races and of the worlds to come. The memory of the stars beat strong in their breasts, gentle eyes, strong love, and passionate, true hearts.

May we awaken and create now, in wise love, my friends, and remember we are sacred, magical beings. We are those queens and kings in unity, harmony, balance and peace, creating new worlds again, with agility, wisdom and ease.

We are becoming a consolidated and unified expression of many souls within one soul. Each one is independent, but also merged in the wholeness of sacred marriage.

The way I see duality is that pre-creation or source energy wanted to experience something other than a non-differentiated state so it became two separate energies: male and female (yin and yang). That expression was allowed to expand for eons until the end of the 26,000-year cycle of time. Should these separate energies keep expanding, as is the nature of the universe, they would possibly have reached a point of no return, like a rubber band that would break if overstretched. Perhaps the creative male-female energy has had enough of separation and has begun to spring back to its whole state of being. Thus, we, as the expression of these dual energies, are coming back together in unity and one accord as twin flames. The feminine (Sophia) and masculine (Christos) are reuniting in each sacred marriage within each of us. We are all twin flames to one another and to all of creation. To borrow a phrase from the 1960s, I say, it is time we "make love, not war." We are beginning to make etheric love to one another as we connect our hearts, minds, and spirits.

Peace is not the absence of chaos. Peace is about maintaining calmness in the midst of the storm. When we stand calmly at the cross point of the infinity symbol, we create a resonant field that will allow us to create something new. There we will know that whatever we believe can and will be true for us. We are *not* few in numbers. We are the *many* and we are powerful in our capacity to love our way into a wonderful new creation. The few are running amuck and grasping at straws to keep the old paradigm intact.

This is not a time for the faint of heart, nor a time to simply read or talk about light language, ascension, and holding resonate fields. This is a time of action. We have the tools, skill sets, and help from those in body and galactic being in other forms. Let us move forward, making cosmic love to ourselves and every person, in every moment.

As our personal and collective gridline systems come into oneness with Source and we step into a new level of our multidimensional selves, new levels of physical, emotional, and mental healing will arise. Similar to what stem cell technology promises, our higher-frequency self brings divine intelligence to renew every function of our body on every level—all the cells, the DNA, brain, emotions, etc. We will not only heal from genetic diseases, deformities, illnesses, and injury, we will be able to regenerate limbs and organs. Soon, we will be able to communicate soul to soul through the multidimensional light that carries unconditional love, divine creativity, and infinite knowing. When we communicate in this way, we share our light with one another.

I realize it is hard to trust anyone with a new idea—although light language is not new. I suggest you keep an open mind and then decide if it is useful for you on your spiritual path. If it does not seem to work at first, don't give up too quickly. If I had given up on writing light code, I would have missed the gift of being able to provide galactic readings with it.

> *Rejoice always, pray continually, give thanks in all*
> *circumstances . . . Do not quench the Spirit. Do not*
> *treat prophecies with contempt but test them all;*
> *hold on to what is good, reject every kind of evil. (I*
> *Thessalonians 5: 16-22)*

Codes are activated through light language and vibration of sound. The more people who speak and tone the light, the more rapidly the codes open. If you feel an urge to speak light language, give it a try. I encourage you to speak light language as much as possible. Aloud is best due to the vibration it carries; but, there are many ways you can express the language of light.

My prayer is for light codes to be activated in you and on all levels of your beautiful being. And, may light language come forth in everyone seeking higher love and purer consciousness on this planet. Doing so will help to dissolve and transmute the greed and fear that has controlled the masses for eons on Earth. May we heal our bodies, mend relationships, bring peace to families, and awaken spiritual gifts through the activation of our spiritual birthright, the restoration of our divine DNA.

Can you imagine the benefit, individually and collectively, if the attributes of awareness, presence, and intent could be accessed easily while driving, shopping, or just moving through crisis or obstacles during your everyday experience? The human form was specifically created to do just that and has the capability of remembering it easily. From my experience, being in the physical presence of a few people can create a resonate field (which is our natural movement) much stronger than when just one person is holding the vibration. If two or more people can come together as alchemists of change and influence the vibrational energy of a room, just imagine what could happen to human consciousness if thousands of people did so regularly.

If the frequencies of like-minded people with divinely intended vibrational thought are focused toward creating Heaven on Earth, we could transform the destruction and depopulating of the planet and change the fabric of our world. It is being done in many locations and by ordinary people who have remembered the skill sets that bring resonance. When we, individually, move in a resonant field we become part of the larger field of unlimited possibilities. We become part of the change by simply maintaining and sustaining our personal field of resonance and joining with others in the "field." This process is being done by people around the globe. As we come together in our awareness of our multidimensional selves, we are joining and linking our "pockets of awareness." We are taking this awareness into our homes, workplaces, schools, and business. Blessed be!

In closing, I offer the paraphrased words of a song written by Charles H. Gabriel:

Send the light, the blessed Cosmic light;
Let it shine from shore to shore!
Send the light, the blessed Cosmic light;
Let it shine forevermore!

May grace everywhere abound, and a Christ-like spirit everywhere be found!

About the Author

Yvonne Perry is an author, coach, and galactic ambassador who offers compassionate healing, intercession, and activation of light language through her books, workshops, and speaking engagements.

As an empath and a starseed walk-in, Yvonne accesses the wise guidance of her higher self, the angelic and fae kingdoms, ascended masters, galactic beings of light to bring energy for healing and activation. During her sessions, she incorporates earth and animal medicine to help people shift into wholeness and integrate multidimensional aspects of their souls.

Holding a Bachelor of Science in Metaphysics from the American Institute for Holistic Theology, she understands the "homecoming" or ascension process. Her participation in fundamentalist religions (and subsequent healing after leaving organized religions) gives her an understanding of the mental and emotional stress that this kind of indoctrination can create for people. As a shaman, Yvonne travels between worlds to restore parts of the soul, which may have fragmented during trauma.

Yvonne is helping to activate people into living an authentic life of wholeness and oneness. Those who are ascending into purer consciousness will find comfort, information, and support to take the next step on this beautiful journey of light.

See http://weare1inspirit.com for more information or to learn about the other books Yvonne has written.

Works Cited

Chapter 1:

1. Caroll, Suzan Ph.D. "Arcturian Corridor Step 15 Downloading ilght Language." Multidimensions.com. <http://www.multidimensions.com/CommPortal/commportal_arc2_s tep15.html>.

Chapter 3:

1. Whitfield, Joseph. <u>The Treasure of El Dorado</u>. Chapter 7. The Bodies of Man. EXCERPTS from dictated communications by Ascended Masters.

Chapter 4:

1. DeMarco, Terri. "The Language of Light." November 9, 2010. Accessed 17 February 2014. <http://www.soulenergyheals.com/apps/blog/show/5286143>.

Chapter 6:

1. Mort, Shely. "The Languages of Creation Light Language or Star Languages." 2004. Accessed 17 January 2014. <http://www.expandingrealities.net/lightlanguage.htm>.

2. Cushman, Dr. Arthur. Facebook and email correspondences. 2 January 2014.

Bibliography

"Brainwaves and State of Consciousness." Psychic101.com. Accessed 12 February 2014. <http://www.psychic101.com/brainwaves-beta-alpha-delta.html>.

"The Lost Books of the Bible Onsite The Book of Enoch." Bibleufo.com Accessed 17 February 2014. <http://www.bibleufo.com/anomlostbooks61.htm>.

"Glossolalia." Wikipedia.com. Accessed 17 February 2014. <http://en.wikipedia.org/wiki/Glossolalia>.

"The Book of Enoch." HeavenlyNet.net. 24 July 2013. Accessed 19 February 2014. <http:// Heavennet.net/writings/the-book-of-enoch/>.

"United States incarceration rate." Wikipedia.com. Accessed 17 February 2014. <http://en.wikipedia.org/wiki/United_States_incarceration_rate >.

"Xenoglossy." Wikipedia.com. Accessed 17 February 2014. <http://en.wikipedia.org/wiki/Xenoglossy> .

Amenreu. In-person interview. January 2014. Email correspondence. January 2014.

Anomellarun, Astelle. Facebook correspondence. Email correspondence. January and February 2014.

Bauman, Dirksen (2008). Open Your Eyes: Deaf Studies Talking. University of Minnesota Press.

Beavers, Kelly. Email correspondence. January and February 2014.

Bray, Jess. Skype interview. January 2014.

Caroll, Suzan Ph.D. "Arcturian Corridor Step 15 Downloading ilght Language." Multidimensions.com.

<http://www.multidimensions.com/CommPortal/commportal_arc2_step1 5.html>.

Chopra, Deepak, MD, and Rudolph E. Tanzi, Ph.D. "Big Idea 2014: You Will Transform Your Own Biology." 10 December 2013. Accessed 27 January 2014. <www.linkedin.com/today/post/article/20131210130858-75054000-big-idea-2014-you-will-transform-your-own-biology>.

Cushman, Dr. Arthur. Facebook and email correspondences. 2 January 2014.

de Vito, Doug. "The Axiatonal Lines." sey-yes.com. Accessed 14 February 2014. <http://www.sey-yes.com/axiatonal.html>.

DeMarco, Terri. "The Language of Light." November 9, 2010. Accessed 5 January 2014. <http://www.soulenergyheals.com/apps/blog/show/5286143>.

Fruchtenbaum, Arnold G. "The Toronto Phenomenon (Part 1 of 2)." 1997. Accessed 6 January 2014. <http://www.deceptioninthechurch.com/96a-03.htm>.

Gabriel, Charles H. "Send the Light." TimelessTruths.org. Accessed 10 January 2014. <http://library.timelesstruths.org/music/Send_the_Light>.

Hall, Jennifer. Phone interview. January 2014. Email correspondence. January 2014.

Hodgson, Alison. Facebook correspondence. January 2014.

Luasa, Mara. "What is the Language of Light?" CelticHeartsHealing.com. Accessed 17 February 2014. <http://www.celtich Earthealing.com/light-language--sacred-sound.html>.

Mazuin Mynrose. Facebook correspondence. January and February 2014.

Morningstar, Diana. Email correspondences. 2 January 2014.

Mort, Shely. "The Languages of Creation Light Language or Star Languages."
2004. Accessed 17 January 2014.
<http://www.expandingrealities.net/lightlanguage.htm>.

Nelson, Betsy. In-person meeting, 17 January 2014. Email correspondences.

O'Grady ,Veronica. Email correspondence. January and February 2014.

Price, Jamye. Email correspondence. February 2014.

Progeny, Angi Gaian. Facebook correspondence. January and February 2014.

Savino, Maryanne. Email Interview. 14 January 2014. Phone Interview. 20
January 2014.

Singleton, Emily. Email Correspondences. January and February 2014.

Stanley, Dr. Salo. Email correspondence. 3 February 2014.

Tinus, Teri Jo. Facebook correspondence. January 2014.

Vara Humphreys. Email correspondences. January and February 2014.

White, Paul. "The Secrets of Thoth and The Keys of Enoch." October 1999.
Accessed 17 February 2014.
<http://www.bibliotecapleyades.net/enoch/esp_enoch_6.htm>.

Williams, Brenda. Email correspondences. Phone interviews. January and
February 2014.

Woodward, TJ. "Shift Happens." YouTube.com. Accessed 10 February 2014.
<http://www.youtube.com/watch?v=x2JlxcCSwQw>.